PISH-LA-KI

PISH-LA-KI

THE LOST MERRICK
AND MITCHELL SILVER MINE

By

James H. Knipmeyer

aventine press

All photos by James H. Knipmeyer unless otherwise indicated.

Cover photo: Prospector monument
Across Piute Canyon to Navajo Mountain

Author photo, back cover: Courtesy of Harvey Leake

Published by Aventine Press
55 E. Emerson St.
Chula Vista CA, 91911

ISBN: 978-1-59330-983-1

Printed in the United States of America

Table of Contents

Introduction

The Lost Merrick and Mitchell Silver Mine, or as it is often called by its Navajo name, the Pish-la-ki Mine, is one of the best known of the many "lost" mines seemingly to dot the wide-flung landscape of the American Southwest. A simple search on Google of either of the two names will turn up a host of sites concerning it. Accounts of the mine, ranging from but a brief mention of a few sentences to entire chapters, have appeared in scores of magazines and books since the beginning of the 1900s. The Pish-la-ki has truly taken on a nearly legendary status, not only to lost mine and treasure enthusiasts, but to more serious historians and scholars as well.

However, with this notoriety has come both embellishments and sensationalism. One often-published writer of the 1960s even went so far as to call the Merrick and Mitchell lode the "most lied about mine in the West." But he himself was probably the most prolific storyteller to do just that. There have been accounts of not just one but three generations of Merricks associated with the mine, and even the discovery of ancient maps in the dusty basements of old Mexican churches. But all are without any basis in fact.

In many instances, though, it is not outright lying, but simply the carrying on and retelling of previous errors and mistakes in the mine's story by later authors. While the Navajo name of the mine, Pish-la-ki, is the Anglicized corruption of the Navajo word *béésh lagai'*, meaning "whitish-colored metal," or simply "silver," the English name Merrick-Mitchell is not so definite as it may seem. Even in recent years a highly respected researcher and author of several well-acclaimed books on various aspects of the history of the American Southwest, made the statement that "What is known about James Merrick and Ernest Mitchell, beyond their names and last few hours, is little indeed." Subsequent research, however, has revealed that with the exception of the last name Mitchell, the other three names are all incorrect.

Indeed, the seemingly simple fact of the mine being silver has not always been clear-cut either. While the decade of the 1880s consistently referred to it as a silver mine, beginning in the early 1890s and continuing until after 1900, it was just as often associated with gold. This was probably due to the influence of the 1892-93 San Juan gold excitement along that river in southeastern Utah.

Therefore, it is the intent of this book to gather together and present the known history of the Pish-la-ki mine, from its presumed earliest discovery in the 1860s until continued searches for it well into the 20th century. And, hopefully, some of the inaccuracies in the story of the Merrick and Mitchell mine will also be corrected.

James H. Knipmeyer
May, 2020

One:
Hashkéneinii

The story of the Pish-la-ki mine actually has its beginning back in 1864. For well over a century before that time, there had been almost continual conflict between the Spanish colonists of what would later come to be the present-day state of New Mexico, and the Native American Navajo. *Diné* (the Navajo name for themselves, meaning "The People") raiders from the west would periodically swoop down on the Rio Grande settlements or other outlying villages, where they would drive off horses and other stock and occasionally capture young children and women as well. The Spanish, in turn, would then mount punitive forays back into *Dinétah*, the Navajo homeland, and take their own share of captives for slaves and servants. These back-and-forth retaliatory actions continued following Mexico's independence from Spain in 1821, and even after the 1848 acquisition by the United States of the territory making up today's Arizona and New Mexico. With the American takeover, however, larger and more organized military reprisals were initiated. The U.S. troop commanders even began to utilize Utes, longtime enemies of the Navajo, as mercenary allies. To the *Diné* this period came to be known as *Náhonzhoodáá'*, the "Fearing Time."

In 1862, Brigadier General James H. Carleton was made commander-in-chief of the U.S. military's Department of New Mexico. With the Army's failure in the preceding years to deliver a decisive military defeat to what amounted to a guerilla-type warfare on the part of the Navajos, Carleton implemented a new, two-part plan in 1863. The first was his now-infamous "scorched earth policy." Led in the field by Colonel Christopher "Kit" Carson, during the winter of 1863-64, troops concentrated on the burning and destruction of the fields, orchards, and dwellings of the Navajo people, as well as the capture or killing of their horses and sheep. This effectively deprived them of their basic livelihood. This policy was carried on even beyond *Dinétah*, into Arizona territory to the Canyon de Chelly and Chinle Valley areas, and by late 1864 ultimately still farther west. Subsequently, with the surrender of scores, then hundreds, and finally even thousands of *Diné*, the Navajos were marched eastward under guard and placed in captivity in an area known as *Bosque Redondo*. This was located in the Pecos River valley of eastern New Mexico, near Fort Sumner, and fulfilled the second part of General Carleton's plan.

However, not all of the *Diné* submitted to what became known in Navajo lore as the Long Walk. Scattered families and small bands hid out in the rugged canyon and plateau area of what is now northern Arizona, where they scratched out a living in the often barren and harsh landscape. One such band was that of a relatively unimportant "headman" then living near Tyende, the area around today's town of Kayenta. Now known by a later name, Hashkéneinii, in the late fall of 1864, he received word of the approach of American soldiers from the east. Many of the surrounding Navajo people, seemingly giving in to what they perceived as the inevitable, chose to stay and wait for the oncoming troops.

According to the account later related by Hashkéneinii's son, Hashkéneinii Biyé, his father, however, made the decision not to surrender. Some seventeen relatives and a handful of others quickly gathered what was reported to be a score of sheep, three horses, one gun, and a little food, and under the cover of darkness started on their way to the north. Past the towering black spire of Agathla Peak, the fleeing band entered what is now known as Monument Valley. This was, at that time, territory frequented by Utes, and Hashkéneinii and his followers hid out during the day and traveled by night.

After a while the band turned to the west. The country became very rough, and they had to cross several high mesas and deep canyons. Hashkéneinii refused to let them slaughter any of the sheep for food, so the rag-tag bunch was forced to hunt for plant seeds and edible roots to live on. They were headed toward the believed protection of Navajo Mountain, as there were no Utes in that part of the country. Finally, after several days, the band reached the southeast end of the mountain.

Good water and grass were found, and the decision was made to stop there and establish a permanent camp.[1]

The above is the only first-hand account of Hashkéneinii's escape from U.S. troops and subsequent settlement near the foot of Navajo Mountain, its isolated, dome-shaped bulk situated on the border between the present-day states of Arizona and Utah. This story refutes some of the more modern, popular stories of Hashkéneinii and, ultimately the Merrick-Mitchell silver mine, concerning those same events. These newer tales have the fleeing Navajos staying just one step ahead of the pursuing soldiers, before becoming seemingly trapped at the banks of the San Juan River. Then, dramatically, the desperate natives ford the rising waters just before the arrival of their pursuers, who by then find the swollen stream too deep to cross. Frustratingly blocked for several days, when the river finally does subside, the Navajos are safely far away on the opposite side. The now escaped band is led by Hashkéneinii westward, before doubling back across the San Juan farther downstream and heading south toward the safety of Navajo Mountain.[2]

While these later stories are plausible enough as far as the geography and terrain are concerned, it must be questioned why Hashkéneinii Biyé would leave out these seemingly important details in his account. The crossing of the San Juan River, which in those times was seldom done by the *Diné*, would surely have rated mention. And while they are admittedly incomplete as to some dates, the existing military reports of the various U.S. troop movements covering this time period fail to mention any such pursuit of Navajos to the banks of the San Juan River.

Hashkéneinii's escape to the north, and then west, can easily be matched with the surrounding countryside and known native trails. Just a few miles north of Agathla Peak, the enclosing sandstone plateau and mesas open out to the west and allow easy access to the Oljeto area and what is now called Copper Canyon. A long-used Native American trail then, and still does, lead west over and across intervening mesas and canyons. Known as the *Ooljéé'tóh*, or Moonlight Water trail, it heads in a generally westward direction directly to Navajo Mountain.

The place where Hashkéneinii and his band finally settled could well have been along today's Cottonwood Wash, which does indeed wind its way in a southeasterly direction from the foot of Navajo Mountain.

11

At one place in particular, springs well up from the often-dry wash, and create a greener, grass-covered area surrounded by cottonwood trees. Called by its *Diné* name of *T'iis yaa tóh*, "Water Under the Cottonwoods," it was this site in the late 1920s that gave rise to the establishment of the Dunn, or Navajo Mountain Trading Post.

That first winter Hashkéneinii still would not allow any of their sheep to be used for food. As Hashkéneinii Biyé described in his later interview, his father made everyone gather berries, grass seed, and roots. They also undoubtedly hunted small game animals. He made everyone work hard every day, and his people got seemingly little rest. It was at this time that they gave him the name *Hashkéneinii*, most often rendered in English as Hoskininni, and meaning the "Angry One," because he doled out their meager food supply in a very strict and disciplined way.[3]

To the *Diné*, Navajo Mountain is known as *Naat'sis'aan*, "Head of Earth Woman," one of their assemblage of holy personages. Hashkéneinii and his band remained near the foot of their protecting mountain for almost five years. During this period of time they slowly increased the size of their sheep herd, acquired horses during forays into the surrounding country, and ultimately had plenty of food and hides and wool for blankets and clothing. One day Hashkéneinii was out hunting on the mountain and, according to his son, found a place where there was silver in the rocks. He brought some of it back to camp, and they pounded it into jewelry. Soon everyone had plenty of silver for ornaments for their belts and saddles. Only six other men, besides Hashkéneinii himself, knew the location of the outcrop.[4] The seeming ease of working the silver found by Hashkéneinii has led some later writers to believe that the metal was a relatively pure form known as native, or horn silver.[5]

Midway through the year 1868, a treaty was made between the United States and the Navajo people which called for the establishment of a Navajo Indian Reservation. Six *Diné* headmen at the internment camp at Bosque Redondo signed the peace pact for the entire Navajo people, and the some eight thousand former prisoners were now set free to return to their homeland. By the following year many of those natives who had lived in the Tyende area finally straggled back there. Word of this soon reached Hashkéneinii, and he and his followers ultimately also returned to their former home. While most of the returning *Diné* had little but the clothes on their backs, Hashkéneinii's people, in comparison, were considered rich, with their large herds of sheep and horses and much silver. Hashkéneinii, because of this wealth and accompanying influence, soon became the leader not only of the immediate Tyende area, but eventually the entire Monument Valley region as well.

During the next decade Hashkéneinii's Navajos would sometimes travel far afield; to the newly established Tuba City to the southwest, north across the Colorado River to the Mormon settlements in Utah, and even, on occasion, to the trading posts and mining camps on the upper San Juan in Colorado. At these places the white trading post operators and townspeople would closely regard the richly laden *Diné*, with their silver rings, bracelets, and necklaces, and their silver ornamented saddles and bridles. They knew that these natives did not trade for their silver, so they began to assume that the Navajo must have a secret silver mine, hidden somewhere deep in their rock-bound territory.[6]

Thus was born the legend of the Pish-la-ki mine.

Hashkéneinii, 1909
Courtesy of Harvey Leake, Wetherill Collection

Navajo Mountain, Southeast side

Two:

Myrick, aka Merrick, aka Merritt

According to faulty legend, and even faultier research, the name of the first white man to discover the Pish-la-ki mine, or at least locate samples of its ore, has been most often given as James Merrick. However, more thorough research has revealed that neither the given or surname is accurate. It may be noted, then, that the subtitle of this book, as well as various references in the Introduction, use the name Merrick simply as a convenience due to its overwhelmingly common usage and familiarity.

The correct name should actually be Charles S. Myrick. The proof of this is the signing of his name to a letter dated December 24, 1879, just a few days before his departure from the Henry L. Mitchell ranch on the San Juan River on his last quest for the Navajo silver mine.[1] Subsequent letters from Mr. Mitchell in early and mid-February of 1880 gave his name as "Merritt," evidently a misunderstanding of Myrick's last name.[2] A newspaper article in the latter part of February of the same year printed the name as "Merrick," presumably a slight mispronunciation of Myrick.[3] Unfortunately for future historians and writers, these two names have continued to be used in nearly every instance even up until the present decade.

Also in modern times the first name James has been consistently used in many published materials concerning the Pish-la-ki mine.[4] This inaccuracy perhaps stems from the use of the name "James Merritt" by Andrew Jenson, Assistant Historian of the Church of Latter-day Saints, in 1917.[5] However, study of the earliest contemporary accounts of the silver mine, from 1880 through 1883, reveal the equally consistent use of the name Charles Myrick.[6] For historical accuracy then, this name will be used from this point foreward.

Nothing is known about Myrick's early life. His age in 1879-80 was estimated to be somewhere in his 40s.[7] According to Cass Hite, longtime miner in the Glen Canyon region of south-central Utah and also one of the hopeful searchers for the fabled Pish-la-ki mine in the early years of the 1880s, Myrick was a "Prescott, Arizona, miner."[8] Hite, a contemporary of Myrick's, should have known, as he himself prospected around the Prescott area in the mid-1870s before moving on farther northeast to the recently established mining camp of Rico, in southwestern Colorado, later in 1879.

Myrick may also have left Prescott around this time, joining the wave of other prospectors wending their way toward the San Juan Mountains and the new mining town there. This is probably why he is called a "Colorado prospector" and a "prospector in the mines of Colorado" in later writings about the Pish-la-ki mine.[9]

Other modern accounts maintain that Myrick was a soldier with Carson's troops during the Navajo's Long Walk to Fort Sumner in 1864-65. In this version of the story he noticed the natives' many silver ornaments and jewelry and wondered just where the source of all of this precious metal was to be found.[10]

Though Myrick's age would perhaps support his being a member of the U.S. Army in the mid-1860s, other details do not bear closer scrutiny. The Navajos as a whole did not begin widespread fashioning of silver jewelry until after their incarceration at Bosque Redondo. Even what little jewelry they may have had at that time was probably not openly worn for fear of "confiscation" by the escorting white soldiers. Lastly, of the some eight thousand *Diné* released in 1868, Myrick would have had little or no idea which group to follow to their supposed mine, as they literally scattered to the four winds into the hundreds of square miles of their homeland.

Whether soldier or miner, a Rico newspaper in March of 1880 stated that Myrick had first visited the area of the Pish-la-ki mine some nine years earlier but had been driven away by the local Indians. Six years later he ventured in a second time but was once again compelled to leave. Finally, after his most recent exploration in the Navajo country in 1879, the persistent prospector now returned to the new mining camp of Rico, where he gave glowing accounts of the richness of the mineral he had found.[11]

Though most modern, popular accounts tell only of Myrick's last two trips to the area of the Pish-la-ki mine, it seems that he actually made at least a handful of explorations in that region. This is echoed in Cass Hite's 1883 newspaper article, in which he says that Myrick had made "several" expeditions into the Navajo country.[12]

In 1892, Porter Mitchell, one of the sons of Henry L. Mitchell, gave an extensive interview concerning the Pish-la-ki mine. In 1879 he was still living at the family home and settlement on the San Juan River when Myrick passed through. Mitchell said that Charles Myrick, with "an uncle," first came from a prospecting tour in California about 1875. When Navajo Mountain was reached, they found coarse metallic ore and brought out rich samples with them. Then, sometime in 1879, Myrick, this time with "one Jones", returned to the region of Navajo Mountain to prospect further. On this occasion rich silver bodies were located east of, but near, the mountain. They then returned to Mitchell's ranch and the upper San Juan settlements of southwest Colorado. At the end of 1879, Myrick left once again for Navajo Mountain, this time inducing a younger brother of Porter Mitchell to come with him.[13]

The "uncle" mentioned by Porter Mitchell remains a complete mystery. The only other reference to this uncle was made during an interview with James M. Rush, Jr. in 1934. In 1879 Rush was a young, seventeen-year-old resident of the little town of Mancos, Colorado, when Myrick passed through with his samples of silver ore. At that time Myrick supposedly related that "his uncle," while traveling to California by way of Lee's Ferry on the Colorado River, had found a rich silver mine along the way.[14] The name of this uncle was either not given by Myrick or was not remembered by Rush, who was of course speaking some fifty-five years after the fact.

At least one later writer evidently seized upon the obscure mention of "an uncle" in Porter Mitchell's 1892 interview and concocted what can only be termed a wildly imaginative story about him. In a magazine article printed in 1966 and written under the pseudonym of John R. Winslowe, this writer stated that in 1855 the first Myrick, the uncle, had somehow obtained a map of what he called a gold mine, which had been copied from a document found in an ancient mission church. This is a fortuitous happenstance that occurs in many such "lost mine" stories.

And as also happens in many of these fanciful accounts, Myrick and his subsequently recruited search party were suddenly attacked by Indians while at or near the mine. Only Myrick and two others escaped back to California.

Age and infirmity kept this first Myrick from ever returning to the mine, but before he died he told the secret to his brother, John. In 1876 this second Myrick and sixteen men found their way to the mine, but, and certainly straining credulity, they too were attacked by Indians. This time, but not surprisingly by now in the story, Myrick was the only survivor. Back home, however, he could enlist no others to go back with him for another try. Finally, he told the facts to the third Myrick, his son Robert, who soon did make a successful trip and obtained at least some of the mine's rich ore. According to this account, this was the Myrick who then took those samples to the towns and mining camps of southwest Colorado and who eventually teamed up with a son of Henry Mitchell for one last foray into the dangerous and deadly Navajo country.[15]

"Gladwell "Toney" Richardson, the actual name of the author of the above piece of fiction, was a prolific writer and contributor to many of the "pulp Western" magazines that were widely popular during the 1960s and 1970s. He and his family and various in-laws had been actively engaged in the operation of several trading posts on the Navajo Indian Reservation from the 1920s up until the 1960s. Richardson was therefore familiar with the land, its peoples, and its history, all of which form the background of many of his articles. In the majority of these, however, there seems to be a lost mine or buried treasure in almost every hillside and under nearly every bush of the canyon and plateau region. Richardson was a firm believer in the adage to never let the facts get in the way of a good story.

According to more substantive accounts, in 1879, George W. Spencer lived with his family in Animas City, one of the southwestern Colorado mining communities. In a manuscript written years later, his son, Arthur H. Spencer, said that there were two prospectors by the name of Myrick and Mitchell. Myrick stayed at Heffernan's place when in town, and Mitchell stayed at the hotel. They went down into the Navajo Mountains, found a silver vein, and came out with a load of samples. They left a sack of the ore at the Spencer house and, since Mr. Spencer was a mining engineer, he had it assayed. Reportedly the sample ran 200 ounces of silver to the ton. The two prospectors said that they would soon be returning to the source of the silver to stake their claims.[16]

However, in neither a conversation later attributed to Myrick or any of the various accounts given by the Mitchells, is it ever mentioned that any of Mitchell's sons accompanied Myrick except on his last trip. Arthur Spencer wrote the above story some sixty years after the fact, and no doubt at that late time only recalled the name of the much better-known Mitchell. It is very likely, therefore, that it was, in fact, Porter Mitchell's "one Jones" who was Myrick's companion on the earlier prospecting venture.

Jones was first mentioned as early as March of 1880, not long after Myrick's last and fatal journey. A newspaper article stated that Myrick was accompanied on the earlier trip by another man, whose name was given as "__ __ Jones." It further said that the two were on their way from California to Arizona, headed toward the northeast, when they discovered what they thought to be a very rich silver mine. They took some of the ore and brought it with them to the settlements on the upper San Juan River in southwest Colorado. Myrick remained in the area for a few weeks before leaving for the Navajo country once again. But Jones, however, was still there.[17]

In the next year or so, Jones was evidently persuaded to guide later prospecting parties in search of Myrick's silver prospect, but to no avail. It was finally bluntly stated that Jones was so easily turned about that he would completely lose himself in the seeming maze of canyons and mesas.[18]

This Jones was undoubtedly James L. Jones. A J.L. Jones was a co-signer of a letter written by San Juan settler Henry L. Mitchell on December 24, 1879. Significantly, Charles S. Myrick was also one of the other co-signers.[19] A delinquent tax list that was published in a Durango newspaper in 1883, also included earlier yearly lists. The name J.L. Jones appears in that for 1880.[20] Finally, in the 1880 U.S. Federal Census for the State of Colorado, the McElmo District on the San Juan River, though actually located in southeastern Utah, was also included because of its proximity and close relationship with Colorado. In that census record is listed a James Jones, age 36, and who boarded, significantly enough, with Henry L. Mitchell.[21]

Although written some two years later, a January 1882 article in one of the Durango newspapers provided some additional details about the silver strike found by Myrick and Jones in 1879. It said that the "lode" was in a canyon near Navajo Mountain. While camped near its brink, Myrick had gone down for water and made the discovery. He then brought along a gunny sack and filled it with several pounds of what turned out to be rich ore.[22]

In Porter Mitchell's interview, he stated that the silver ore was found east of and near Navajo Mountain. He further went on to say that the ore lay in ledges "of some thickness," and that the Indians dug out the silver from under the rocks.[23]

While in many of the above instances the writer or speaker may very well have gotten their facts from Myrick or Jones, it is never specifically stated that this was the case. There is one account, however, when the informant did get his facts directly from Myrick himself. While traveling from the Utah towns west of the Colorado River to the new Mormon settlement of Fort Montezuma on the San Juan River, George B. Hobbs met both Myrick and Mitchell on December 29, 1879, and once again on the 31st. Sometime later, dictating an account of his excursions during that winter of 1879-80, Hobbs repeated a conversation that he had with Myrick on the latter date. He said that the prospector told him that "about a year before," he had passed from Fort Wingate, in New Mexico, to Lee's Ferry, on the Colorado River in northern Arizona. While going through the "Navajo Nation" he had discovered three crude smelters, where the Indians had been smelting silver from ore which later assayed at 90% silver. He was going to try and find those mines.[24]

The fact that it was only smelters which had been found by Myrick, and not the actual mine itself, was further verified by a statement just a few months later in the Rico newspaper. Several smelters of stone construction had been found in the Navajo country, and some of the ore which had been brought away was found to be nearly pure silver.[25]

Myrick's brief and unadorned statement of the facts is most likely the closest to being accurate and the truth. No matter what even some contemporary accounts may have said, he had not as yet found the mine itself. He had found but three so-called smelters. He had recovered some specimens of ore from them and was now only returning for more samples. And that was the extent of it.

Charles S. Myrick 1879 signature
National Archives & Records Administration

Three:

Mitchell

When Myrick and Jones came back from their mid-1879 venture into the Navajo country, the first white settlement that they encountered was the Mitchell ranch. This was on the north side of the San Juan River near the mouth of McElmo Creek and across from what was considered the domain of the Navajo to the south. In January of 1879 the extended Mitchell clan had migrated down the McElmo from the Montezuma Valley in the southwest corner of Colorado. By December of that year some seventy people, men, women, and children, were said to reside in the immediate area. The Mitchell family itself, and their in-laws, made up the majority of that number. Here on the San Juan, Henry L. Mitchell, patriarch of the clan, also had, while not a true trading post, a small store to serve the surrounding settlers and travelers passing through the area.

After undoubtedly recouping for a brief time at the Mitchell settlement, Myrick and Jones soon left for the mining towns of southwest Colorado, there to look for potential backers and investors, but also to recruit additional companions to go back to the Navajo country and establish actual claims. According to later accounts, this took them to several San Juan Mountain settlements and mining centers.

Clarence A. "Alfred" Frost, in a 1960 letter, said that a man named Joe Duckett had at one time told him that in 1879 he was running a small store on the San Juan River, where Montezuma Creek comes in from the north. While there a man named Myrick came by with very good samples of ore before going on to Mancos, Colorado.[1]

Frost was but a youth from Monticello, Utah, when he visited with Joe Duckett, who at that time was an elderly man living in nearby Verdure Canyon. He did not write his 1960 letter for some decades after that encounter. Therefore, it is not surprising that Frost got a few of his facts wrong. In late 1879 the only settlement of any kind at the mouth of Montezuma Creek with the San Juan River was what was charitably referred to as Fort Montezuma. This was the nucleus of a proposed Mormon colonizing effort in southeastern Utah and at that time consisted of only two families and two other Mormon individuals. There was certainly no need for any sort of store, however small. Duckett, then, was most likely working at the Mitchell store, a few miles upriver at the mouth of McElmo Creek. This is borne out in a still later rendition of this same story by Frost, when he stated that Duckett had a friend named Mitchell with him.[2]

Frost, however, did get the fact right that the prospector, Myrick (and Jones), was indeed on his way towards Mancos, Colorado. In 1898, Oen E. "Edgar" Noland, at that time a San Juan River trading post operator and resident of Mancos, said that Myrick had discovered his mine during the summer of 1879 and brought ore from it to Mancos. He also added the fact that later it proved to be worth over $600 per ton in silver.[3]

In a 1934 book, Louisa Wade Wetherill, wife of longtime Navajo trader John Wetherill at Oljeto and Kayenta, Arizona, said that in 1879 her father, John J. "Jack" Wade, and his father-in-law, James M. "Martin" Rush, journeyed from Nevada to the Mancos Valley of southwestern Colorado looking at the prospects for a new home. In the fall of that year, the two saw the assays of some samples of mineral ore brought from the Navajo country by a prospector named Myrick. Wade then returned to Nevada for the rest of the family, while Rush stayed on in the valley. The entire Rush-Wade clan arrived back in the Mancos Valley in the spring of 1880. The elder Rush informed them that Myrick had showed him his samples yet again after Jack Wade had left and wanted him to go into a partnership with him in the reported silver mine. But Rush declined, saying that the entire family would soon be on its way from Nevada and that he had to get the crops in beforehand. Like Spencer before her, Mrs. Wetherill also added the fact that the samples, of what turned out to be silver ore, later assayed at $800 a ton. This is $200 more than Spencer's statement but is understandable when it is considered that both accounts were written over fifty years after the actual events took place.[4]

The Mancos connection was confirmed by James M. Rush, Jr., when he stated that Myrick was in Mancos in 1879 and had stayed all night with his father. Rush, Jr. also added the fact that Myrick was on his way to have the ore assayed in Silverton, Colorado.[5]

To reach Silverton, a mining town on the Las Animas River, another north bank tributary of the San Juan, Myrick would have had to pass through the smaller mining community of Animas City. This is confirmed by a statement made by Arthur H. Spencer, longtime prospector and mining speculator, in a manuscript he wrote later in life. He said that in 1879 his family was then living in Animas City, Colorado, when two prospectors stayed in town with samples of ore that assayed 200 ounces to the ton.[6]

In 1946, William "Buck" Lee, who for several years the decade before had run cattle south of the San Juan River near Oljeto, gave an interview with the well-known Mormon archivists, Austin and Alta Fife. He said that along in the late 1860s [sic] there was a prospector named Myrick who came up through the Navajo country headed towards Colorado. At some unidentified place he had found some rocks that were very rich in silver. According to Lee, Myrick took them over to Durango, Colorado, and further averred that the nuggets were still there in a bank vault.[7]

However, in 1879 there was as yet no town of Durango. As the Animas City newspaper stated early the following year, "Only God and the Denver & Rio Grande Railroad know where the proposed town is to be." It was not until the fall of 1880 that the new mining and railroad town was laid out.

A writer in 1949, or just shorty before that, talked with an 89-year-old prospector in Durango and was shown a sample of magnificent silver ore. The elderly gentleman, name not given, said it had been brought back from the Navajo country by a prospector named Myrick. He added that he very much wanted to get a look at that mine, but had a pretty fair gold claim up in the San Juan Mountains in those days and could not afford to get away at the time. The old prospector then concluded by stating, "After I heard what happened to them fellows I figured it was a good thing I couldn't."[8]

Perhaps the assays of the silver were, in fact, made in Silverton, Colorado. But it seems that Myrick's search for possible investors in his mining scheme and also for a number of men to accompany him back to the region of the supposed mine, ultimately took him back to his old stomping ground of Rico, Colorado. In later years, while reminiscing with fellow miner Bert Loper in Glen Canyon of south-central Utah, Cass Hite related that he had first come into the San Juan region hunting for the Pish-la-ki mine. He had been over in Rico, Colorado, when Mitchell and Myrick went into the Navajo country hunting the silver mine the Indians were supposed to have.[9] Cass' brother, Benjamin R. Hite, stated in an 1893 newspaper interview that Cass had even made arrangements to join up with Myrick but was prevented from doing so by business responsibilities.[10]

In several modern-day accounts of Myrick and the Pish-la-ki mine, an individual by the name of Jim Jarvis is portrayed as being a key backer of Myrick. Described as a man of the "Cortez country," he is said to have entered into an agreement with Myrick and staked him to some $4,000. Jarvis then instructed him to go back to his hidden mine and secure more samples. With these to prove that the first ones were not mere chance, he could guarantee that additional investors would be easy to find.[11]

There are, however, a couple of problems with this particular story. First, in 1879 there was not as yet any town of Cortez. While there were at that time several scattered ranches in the Montezuma Valley of southwest Colorado, the community of Cortez would not be established until 1886. Secondly, the only Jim Jarvis then in the region resided in the San Juan Mountain mining town of Telluride, though later he did eventually move down to Durango.[12] Telluride is some twenty-five miles north of Rico across Lizard Head Pass. While it is possible that Myrick journeyed there, it is very unlikely that he would have done so.

While some accounts maintain that Myrick had some difficulty in convincing fellow prospectors to return with him to the Navajo country, in reality that does not seem to have been the case. In another 1893 newspaper interview, Blair Burwell, then a resident of Durango and, like so many others in the region at that time, a onetime searcher himself for the Pish-la-ki mine, said that in 1879 a prospector named Myrick came up to Rico and claimed that he had discovered a rich silver mine. He exhibited some valuable specimens and proceeded to make arrangements for a party to accompany him on a return trip. His story set the mining camp "afire," and he had "no trouble getting his party organized."[13]

Burwell went on to say that Myrick and his party had been gone only a day, however, when "human nature asserted itself" and a general quarrel arose over what share each man was to receive in the mine. Myrick subsequently quit the party in disgust and traveled on alone to the Mitchell settlement on the San Juan.[14]

This last part of the story was repeated by Buck Lee in 1946 during his interview with the Fifes. Though a few details differed, the general outline of the tale was the same. Lee said that in the original agreement made in Rico, Myrick was to be given the right to lay out the first claim. After starting on their way, though, the rest of the party soon decided that he should have to take his chances on making a claim right along with the rest of them. Subsequently, under the cover of darkness, Myrick separated from the others and journeyed alone to Mitchell's place.[15]

Upon arriving at the Mitchell ranch, Myrick must have immediately begun to try and enlist at least one other individual to go along with him to the mine. A story related by Alfred Frost in a book published in 1993, concerned this encounter of Myrick and the Mitchells. This was some thirty-three years after his 1960 letter quoted earlier, and with the passage of additional years even more of the details became scrambled. But essentially the gist of the tale remained the same.

About 1889 [sic], Joe Duckett was employed as a clerk or trader at the Mancos Creek Trading Post [sic], located where the Mancos River entered the San Juan River. As was explained previously, this must actually have been in 1879 at the Mitchell store where McElmo Creek flowed into the San Juan. A friend, Mitchell, was also there. The prospector, Myrick, had had some samples of ore tested, with the result that they showed a high grade of silver. He was now back to return to the Navajo country and obtain a larger sample of ore, in order to persuade men to invest and help mine the silver. Both Duckett and Mitchell wanted to go along, but someone had to stay and take care of the store. It was decided to draw straws to determine who would go, and Mitchell, unfortunately as it would turn out, won.[16]

This, then, was the Mitchell who would accompany Myrick and give his name to the Merrick [sic] and Mitchell silver mine. But of the large family, which Mitchell was it? All accounts over the years agree that it was a son of Henry L. Mitchell. However, most modern stories, since the early 1900s, have incorrectly given the name as Ernest Mitchell. This once again probably stems from the first use of that name by the Assistant Historian of the Mormon Church in 1917.[17] But a simple search of the various U.S. Federal Census Records indisputably shows that this name cannot be accurate.

Henry L. Mitchell and his wife, Caroline, had a total of seventeen children, though not all of them reached adulthood. Of these, nine were boys, and none had the given name of Ernest. To the deserved shame of even some present-day researchers and writers, the correct name of Myrick's new partner was, in fact, correctly used in all of the accounts where it was mentioned, prior to 1917. Though at times variously listed as H.D., Herman, Hernans, and Hernand, all refer to Hernan D. Mitchell, born in 1855, and 24 or 25 years old when he joined with Myrick on his final trip into the Navajo country. While he is shown on the 1870 U.S. Federal Census, significantly he is absent on that of 1880 and later. This 1880 enumeration was made in April of that year, just a little over three months after Mitchell and Myrick had departed on their fateful quest.

Mouth of McElmo Creek

Four:

The Fateful Trip

Myrick and Mitchell left the McElmo settlement sometime just after Christmas, 1879, possibly on the 27th, but more likely on the 28th. They were reportedly riding two horses, with an additional three pack animals well loaded with provisions and bedding.[1]

On the morning of the 29th, the two hopeful prospectors were headed west toward the crossing of Montezuma Creek. Here they encountered four men from the Mormon San Juan Mission, the main body of which was now encamped back on the west side of the Colorado River at what was called Hole-in-the-Rock. More commonly now known as the Hole-in-the-Rock expedition, this large colonizing group was on its way to join the two Mormon families left at Fort Montezuma the preceding year. The four men that Myrick and Mitchell met had been sent on ahead to scout the way across the unknown country between the Colorado River crossing and the infant settlement on the San Juan.

One of the Mormon scouts, George B. Hobbs, had met both Myrick and Mitchell earlier in the year and now stopped for a passing exchange of pleasantries before parting ways. Two days later, after being detained at Fort Montezuma because of heavy rains, Hobbs and his three companions started on the return journey to their waiting party. Just after crossing the Montezuma Wash, they once again ran onto Myrick and Mitchell, who had been driven to shelter in a nearby cabin by the same storms. This time Myrick dropped back to speak privately with Hobbs.

Writing later in his diary, Hobbs said that provided he would keep the secret, Myrick would tell him what he and Mitchell were after – the hidden Navajo silver mine. Myrick was evidently not satisfied with just one man for added protection from possible Indian interference. Therefore, he promised Hobbs that if he would leave his fellow scouts and join them, he would give him one-fourth interest in his discovery, the same as he was giving Mitchell. Hobbs thanked him for the offer, but said that he was duty-bound to return to the waiting colonizing company.

The two groups then traveled on west together until they came to Comb Wash. There they separated, Myrick and Mitchell crossing over to the south bank of the San Juan River.[2]

This was a well-known crossing of the San Juan, later to be known as the Mules Ear Crossing because of the distinctively-shaped sandstone spire rising up from Comb Ridge to the south. The canyon of Chinle Creek led off in that same direction, and a well-used Native American trail followed along and close-by that drainage far into *Diné* country. Where Gypsum Creek entered, another well-beaten trail branched off to the west leading to the Navajos' *Tsé Bii'*, descriptively meaning "Within the Rocks." Later white prospectors called it Monumental Valley, which was eventually shortened to today's Monument Valley.

Just what happened in the next few days has been a matter of speculation and hyperbole for almost a century and a half. Most accounts agree that Myrick and Mitchell made their way back to the area of the mine, or at least to the location where Myrick originally found his samples of ore. There they secured additional pieces of the silver and began their return journey homeward. It is at this point that the controversy begins.

According to William "Buck" Lee, who claimed to have known Hashkéneinii Biyé in the 1930s and perhaps got the story from him, Myrick was riding a bay horse and Mitchell a big mule. They crossed today's El Capitan Creek and started up the trail that leads westward over the mesa. Up there someplace they loaded their bags with silver ore and started on their way back home. Natives of the region discovered the presence of the two prospectors, and after a day's journey they ran into a band of Navajos who had formed an ambush for them as they came down off of the mesa back into Monument Valley. A running fight ensued, and Mitchell was finally shot down at the foot of one of the towering sandstone buttes. The Navajos continued to follow Myrick across the flat desert for a couple of more miles, and finally cornered and killed him by another butte farther to the north.[3]

It was also from Hashkéneinii Biyé that Louisa Wetherill heard the story of how Myrick and Mitchell had been killed. She and her husband, John Wetherill, had run a trading post in the Navajo country at Oljeto since 1906 and more recently at Kayenta beginning in 1910. Louisa became intimately familiar with both Hashkéneinii and his son, as well as most of the *Diné* of the Monument Valley region. Over the years she not only learned the Navajos' language but immersed herself in their culture and history as well. Old Hashkéneinii even adopted the white woman into his clan, believing that she was actually a descendant of an earlier Navajo ancestor. Louisa's version of the story may therefore be more reliable than Buck Lee's.

According to her account, Hashkéneinii Biyé said that, after procuring their additional samples of ore, the two prospectors had returned to Monument Valley. There they stopped at Hashkéneinii's hogan and asked for some mutton to eat. After a sheep had been killed for them they were then directed on to water. After watering their horses and filling their canteens, they rode on to the foot of the butte that was later named for Mitchell and made camp. In the morning they were ready for an early start. A band of local Paiutes had planned a surprise attack on the pair of prospectors at daybreak, but when they came to the men's camp, they found them already mounted.

The Paiutes told them that they had been using Paiute water to which they had no right, but the two white men calmly replied that they were sent to that water by Hashkéneinii. Continued efforts by the natives to pick a fight failed. Finally, one of the Paiutes demanded a chew of tobacco. When Mitchell reached around to his back pocket for a plug of tobacco, the Indian grabbed the gun on his hip. A moment later Mitchell lay dead on the ground, with a bullet from his own gun through his head.

Myrick saw that his partner was shot, so fled for some three miles to the foot of the butte which was later to be named for him. Knowing that he, too, had been wounded, but fearing that he still might have ammunition left for his gun, the Paiute pursuers turned back. Alone among the rocks, Myrick died.[4]

Interestingly, and perhaps giving even more credibility to the above, another version of this same story was printed some sixty-eight years after the appearance of Louisa Wetherill's. Perhaps "version" is really not the correct word to use, as it is almost word for word the same as that published in 1934. However, according to the author, he heard the story one night in the year 1927, and the teller was John Wetherill. Further, he stated that Wetherill himself had first heard it from old Hashkéneinii back in 1909.[5]

In his extensive interview with Charles Kelly in 1939, Hashkéneinii Biyé added some details about the killing of Myrick and Mitchell. He said that two white men, evidently Myrick and Jones, first came into the Navajo country. They found the mine, or ore from it, and took away some samples. In the fall Myrick, this time with young Mitchell, came back again, got some more of the silver ore, and started on their way out. In Monument Valley they met some Utes, who wanted their horses and arms. So, they killed the two men, but left some of their equipment strewn about on the ground.

Hashkéneinii Biyé had seen the tell-tale tracks in the snow that had fallen the night before and followed them until he came upon the site of the attack. He then added the significant statement that there was a Ute, then living around Bluff, Utah, known to the Navajos as No Neck. Hashkéneinii Biyé insisted that this Ute was at the scene and could confirm his story.[6]

Further confirmation of Hashkéneinii Biyé's account came from Arthur H. Spencer. In 1920, during the oil boom in southern Utah along the San Juan River, Spencer was in the Navajo country surveying oil permits and putting up location monuments as the law required. He became acquainted with Hashkéneinii Biyé, who told him that he was herding sheep up on the mesa when Myrick and Mitchell came back from the mine. Hashkéneinii Biyé said that it had snowed during the night, and he ran across their trail. The tracks were of shod horses, meaning that they belonged to white men. Later that day he heard that two whites had been killed.[7]

In several accounts it was Navajos who were said to have killed Myrick and Mitchell, but these seem to rely on purely circumstantial evidence.[8] The two prospectors were in Navajo country; they were looking for a Navajo silver mine; and they were using Navajo water. It was but a case of guilt by association rather than from any hard, more substantial evidence. However, from the very beginning it was Utes, or Paiutes, on whom the blame was cast.

A problem has always existed in distinguishing between Utes and Paiutes in southern Utah and northern Arizona. Slight variations in language, larger differences in lifestyle, overlapping subsistence areas, and especially intermarriage, created a blending of the two groups that exists even until the present day. The San Juan Paiute tribe of southeast Utah and northeast Arizona was, and is, attached to the Weeminuche Ute of southwest Colorado and southeast Utah. These Paiutes have never been accorded full status with the other Ute bands of Colorado and Utah. Even today the Weeminuche band, headquartered at Towaoc, Colorado, and known as the Ute Mountain Utes, are looked down upon by other Ute bands as being a mixture of Ute and Paiute. At the same time the members of the White Mesa Ute band, located just south of Blanding, Utah, who are of Ute-Paiute ancestry, are viewed by those at Towaoc as an even more mixed breed.

The casting of blame on Paiutes was first made almost immediately after the killing of Myrick and Mitchell. In a letter dated only four weeks following the tragic incident, U.S. Indian Agent Galen Eastman, at Fort Defiance, Arizona, penned a report from Boy with Many Horses, one of his best and most trusted Native American scouts. About thirty days earlier, while on a trip into northern Arizona, a Navajo friend had told him that he had been at a Paiute encampment, north toward the San Juan River. There he saw a large black mule, three other pack mules, and other sundry items. The friend further stated that all had been taken by the Paiutes from two white men, who were killed for their animals and equipment by the same Paiutes.[9]

The Ute-Paiute relationship was also first brought up just a matter of weeks after Myrick and Mitchell were slain. In a letter from Captain F.T. Bennett, post commander at Fort Wingate, New Mexico, he reported that one of his informants, Jesus Alviso, a Mexican who lived among the Navajos, had recently been at the Hopi village of Moenkopi in northern Arizona. While there he saw and conversed with five Paiutes. They informed him that it was four Utes from the north side of the San Juan River, but who were married to Paiute women, who had killed the two Americans. The three Utes actually named were "Ozi-jo gachley," his son "Cose-etten," and "Tenneh-Ha-Muzzy." The Paiutes also said that these Utes took two mules and two horses from the Americans.[10]

Even old Henry Mitchell, Hernan Mitchell's father, who at first assumed it was Navajos who had killed his son, finally came around to the belief that Paiutes were actually to blame.[11]

Identification of the three Utes implicated by Captain Bennett's informant is difficult today because the three names were spelled phonetically. Cose-etten may be the Navajo rendering of the Paiute name *Catch-u-we*, known to later Mormon settlers as Big Mouth Mike. Tenneh-Ha-Muzzy is possibly the Paiute later known as Joe Bush.

Albert R. Lyman, one of these Mormon settlers, was a youngster in Bluff, Utah, during the time following the Myrick and Mitchell incident. In later years he gave an interesting, and also very significant, description of the elder Paiute that he called Old Mike: "he with the wide mouth and boar neck...." This obviously was the Big Mouth Mike of earlier years and the No Neck who Hashkéneinii Biyé identified as being at the scene of the Myrick and Mitchell killings. Lyman confirmed this when he said that in later years Old Mike even bragged about being one of the killers of Myrick and Mitchell.[12]

Albert Lyman was reared in and lived in San Juan County, Utah, his entire life. Since childhood he knew and became acquainted with many of the Ute-Paiutes that lived in the White Mesa community south of his home in Blanding. Lyman became especially close to a Paiute whom the whites knew as Posey, and eventually wrote a biography of him. In his book Lyman related the following tale, evidently provided to him by Posey.

Early in January of 1880, the Paiute leader Big Mouth Mike informed his band that two white men had crossed the mesa and come down into Monument Valley from the west. They had a good outfit, six horses and supplies. Posey was thirteen years of age at the time and still called by his adolescent Paiute name of Sowagerie. He said that when Big Mouth Mike and the other adult males took off in pursuit of the two whites, he, curious and wanting in on the action, snuck along after them.

The Paiute pursuers finally sighted the two men at the foot of a high butte, where they had stopped to drink and fill canteens near the hogan of Hashkéneinii. Eventually the two white men were overtaken, and Big Mouth Mike came up alongside the younger of the two men, Mitchell, and demanded a chew of tobacco. When the man leaned forward and twisted around to reach into his back pocket, Mike snatched the pistol from his holster and shot him through the head.

The older man, Myrick, saw his companion slump in the saddle and dashed away. Big Mouth Mike then fired at the fleeing man and wounded him. For four miles Myrick raced, before turning over among the rocks of another large butte. There the Paiutes came up to him, and after he finally died of his wounds, they stripped him of all his clothes and possessions. Posey then significantly added that Hashkéneinii's son, Hashkéneinii Biyé, joined them at about this time.[13]

While these various accounts and stories do differ in a few of their details, such as the exact number of animals that Myrick and Mitchell had with them, and whether they were horses or mules or a combination of each, in the general substance of the tales there is a surprisingly large amount of agreement and confirmation. This is even extended to the identities of two of the prospectors' slayers, Big Mouth Mike and Joe Bush. Albert Spencer said that in the 1930s he had become acquainted with the Indians who had killed Myrick and Mitchell. They were who he called Pah-Ute Mike, and the other was a "Negro-looking Ute" called Joe Bush.[14]

What eventually happened to the animals ridden and driven by Myrick and Mitchell, as well as much of their other equipment, was detailed in a series of official depositions and reports given in 1882. Though two years after the fact, the Myrick and Mitchell incident had at that time once again been brought to the attention of the U.S. Indian Agent at Fort Defiance, Arizona.[15] The most informative of these accounts was that of Alexander M. Stephen, who was employed at the Keams Canyon Trading Post of Thomas V. Keam in northern Arizona from 1879 until 1882.

Stephen stated that early in 1880, the Navajo Agent, Captain F.T. Bennett, had come to Keam's Canyon and held a council with the Navajos and Hopi Indians of the region. During this council some "Northern Navajos" that lived close to the Paiute country near the San Juan River, reported that two Americans had been killed by the Paiutes during the winter of 1879-80. They also said that the Paiutes had mules and firearms belonging to these men.

Captain Bennett then instructed these northern Navajos to obtain possession of the Americans' property and bring it to Mr. Keam at his trading post. He would then reimburse them for any expense they might incur recovering it. Shortly after this council the Navajos brought to Mr. Keam everything belonging to the Americans of which they had any knowledge. They claimed to have paid, in the way of barter with the Paiutes for this property, the amount of $35, which sum Keam then reimbursed the Navajos.

Keam subsequently notified the sheriff of La Plata County, Colorado, that the above-mentioned property was at his place and requested to be advised as to its disposition. The sheriff, in reply, wrote to Keam that

Mr. H.L. Mitchell, who lived on the San Juan River, was the father of one of the men killed, and that the property would be sent for by him as soon as it was practicable to do so.[16]

After Stephen's 1882 deposition, a party was sent out to the north from the Navajo Agency to find and talk with Hashkéneinii, evidently one of the "Northern Navajos" spoken of by Captain Bennett in 1880. One of the members of this party, William Ross, stated that when Hashkéneinii and his band were finally located, Hashkéneinii told them that after Myrick and Mitchell were killed, the Navajos eventually took all of their possessions to Keam's store. However, Keam instructed them not to give up one of the mules until the friends of the dead men paid them a $50 ransom. Hashkéneinii also showed them a gun belonging to the murdered men, and said that Keam had given it to him.[17]

The above was confirmed in every detail by another member of the party, Jonathan P. Williams, the next day after Ross' deposition.[18]

It is interesting here to note that not only at this time but in later years, both Ross and Williams would be key participants in the continued search for the Navajos' Pish-la-ki mine, or, as it was now being more commonly referred to as, the Myrick and Mitchell mine.

Monument Valley

Five:

Search and Burial

Before Myrick and Mitchell departed late in December of 1879 on their quest for additional samples of silver ore, they left instructions on where to look for them if they did not return in a specified amount of time. In subsequent accounts these "instructions" were said to be in the form of a map that Myrick gave to Mitchell's father, and which showed the topography of the country they would be going into.[1] Porter Mitchell, Hernan's older brother, seems to have confirmed this when he stated that if they did not return, searchers were to follow the "course marked out."[2]

The amount of time to await the two prospectors return varies from account to account. Some of these say that a month was allotted.[3] Another stated twenty-five days.[4] Henry L. Mitchell himself, in a letter dated February 5, 1880, merely said that Myrick and his son were to have been back two weeks earlier, which would have been sometime around January 22nd.[5]

Whatever the exact specifications, the two men did not make an appearance within the agreed upon time frame. In yet another letter, this one on February 15, Henry Mitchell indicated that a first search party had already been sent out sometime previous to that date. He added, however, that the two missing men had not been found.[6] That this initial party was unsuccessful is confirmed in a March 16 newspaper article. It said that a party of ten men had set out and looked for some ten days. After that length of time, however, their supplies became exhausted, and they were compelled to return without having found any sign of the two prospectors.[7]

Writing some sixty years after the fact, George P. Schurtz stated that as a youngster in 1879-80 he lived with his family near the Mitchell settlement. He said that this first search party included, besides Mr. Mitchell, Oscar and Michael Shirts, his uncle and older brother. To avoid any undue confusion, although in the 1880s the family spelled their surname Shirts, by the 1930s some branches of the family had gone back to the original German spelling, of Schurtz.

Oscar Shirts later added the names of some of the other men who were with them on this original search: Lee Spaulding, Aaron Stull, and Frank Smith. Significantly, Mr. Schurtz also added the fact that it was not just a shortage of provisions that prompted the first party's return, but that they had also had trouble with the Indians and had come back for additional help.[8]

Six of the returning party remained at Mitchell's ranch, while two of them, O.B. Jackson and I.W. Bradford, went on up to the Mancos Valley to try and get a few more volunteers to join in a new search. They succeeded in recruiting an additional eight men, two of whom were cattlemen Henry C. Goodman and Charles A. Frink.[9] However, before they could get back to Mitchell's, six of the eight men who had remained there had grown impatient and started out for Monumental Valley some six or eight days earlier.[10]

The main party, now once again reduced to ten men, then started out on February 15.[11] Some later accounts give numbers ranging from fourteen to twenty-two men comprising this second search party, or posse, as it was often portrayed.[12] There may have been an additional individual or two from the Mitchell settlement, such as John Y. Carpenter, a son-in-law of Henry Mitchell, who is known to have been a part of this second group.[13] But the significantly larger numbers in these later accounts are actually the result of the authors mistakenly confusing the second search party with a larger prospecting expedition which set out later in the year.

This second search party stayed out almost two weeks, and returned to Mitchell's on the San Juan by February 28. In a letter of that date, Carpenter briefly said that they had just returned from finding the remains of Myrick and Mitchell. The two men had been killed in Monumental Valley, and a Navajo had been hired to take them to the bodies. The Navajos blamed the Paiutes, and the Paiutes blamed the Navajos.[14]

During the ensuing month, in March, several newspaper articles, not only from the San Juan mining town of Rico, Colorado, but also in the Denver tabloids, provided additional details about this search effort.

Mitchell's body had showed but one bullet wound and was found where he and Myrick had camped. Myrick's body, nearly riddled with bullets, was found about three miles from the camp. The Navajos proclaimed innocence and accused the Paiutes.[15]

It appeared that when the two men were attacked, they were fleeing from or trying to avoid coming in contact with any of the local natives. However, they had either accidentally encountered them or were unexpectedly overtaken by the Indians. Mitchell's body was found near their camp, but was very mutilated and torn by coyotes. He could only be recognized by his clothes. One bullet hole was found through the head.

Myrick's body was found about three miles from that of Mitchell. It seemed that he had had a running fight with the Indians, as he was shot eight times through the body. He had dragged himself for some two or three hundred yards through a deep sandy ravine and had crawled under a large overhanging rock. Every twenty or thirty feet patches of dried blood were found by the searchers. His watch remained in his pocket, and his hat and smoke-pipe were located nearby. A lead pencil and pieces of paper were found near his hands, but no writing had been done.[16]

Letters written from the Mancos Valley on February 28 and March 1 were later obtained and published by Denver newspapers. One article said that after four days of travel from the Mitchell ranch, the second search party had reached Monumental Valley. There they found two Indian camps, one of Navajos and the other of a small band of Paiutes. They inquired of the Navajos if they knew of any white men being in the valley near the Blue Mountain, also known as Navajo Mountain. They were told that the nearby Paiutes had killed two men just a few weeks previously.[17]

According to another Denver newspaper, the two letters had been acquired the night of March 15. The search party had encountered a Navajo encampment and learned that Myrick and Mitchell had both been killed. The Navajos also said that it was the Utes, or Paiutes, who had done the killing. The searchers succeeded in hiring a young Navajo, who would show them where the bodies of the two men were.

Mitchell and Myrick were found three to four miles apart. They had evidently been attacked in camp, and Mitchell must have been shot at the very first, as he lay near where the searchers found their saddles and pack-saddles in a little canyon. In this account his clothing showed one bullet hole in the middle of the back, about eight inches below the coat collar, which must have come from behind.

The body of Myrick had not been molested in any way. His clothes showed a number of holes, and evidently six or eight bullets had been sent through his body. One was just under his left eye and had come out at the back of his head. Perhaps this led to the seeming confusion of Mitchell being shot either through the upper back or through the head.

After doing the best they could for the dead men in the way of hasty burials, the search party returned to Mitchell's ranch.[18]

These contemporary accounts in the Rico and Denver newspapers were confirmed in later years by relatives of the participants, Porter Mitchell in 1893[19], Henry Goodman, Jr. in 1934[20], and George Schurtz in 1940.[21] Still other later accounts also added some interesting details that the earlier ones had not.

In 1883, a mere two years after the search and burial party, a short article in one of the Durango newspapers gave a brief description of those events. It also maintained that on the way back to Mitchell's ranch they were visited by a band of Navajos and renegade Paiutes. The natives reportedly acted in a very impudent manner, made threatening gestures toward the whites, and finally indicated that if they did not leave immediately they would all be killed.

It was at this time that Mancos Valley cattleman Henry C. Goodman reportedly rose to the occasion. In what very well could have been a somewhat over-dramatization of the actual event, he supposedly leveled his six-gun at the belly of the leader of the Indian band and warned that if any shooting did begin, he would be the first one to die. The natives then reappraised the situation, backed off, and soon left the premises.[22]

In 1898, representatives of the *Mancos Times* newspaper were shown what was described as "a relic of Indian tragedy" by local resident Oen E. "Edgar" Noland. It was half of a silver dollar with the date 1876 and was said to have been found in the pocket of Hernan Mitchell, when he was killed by Indians in the winter of 1879-80. Edgar Noland was Henry L. Mitchell's son-in-law and the slain man's brother-in-law.

According to Noland's story, Hernan Mitchell was an expert marksman with a rifle. The silver dollar had been neatly cut in two, and one half had been polished and inserted on his gun barrel as a sight. The search party had found what was evidently the other half in his pocket, and it was then brought back and given to his mother. During the past winter of 1897-98, the relic had come into the possession of Mr. Noland.[23]

Yet a third account was contained in a 1910 letter from Mrs. Marion Wetherill, wife of Mancos Valley resident Benjamin K. Wetherill. In it she related that this second search party had also discovered a portion of a quilt near the body of young Mitchell. When they returned to the Mitchell ranch on the San Juan, his mother identified it as part of the quilt that her son had taken with him on his ill-fated journey.[24]

All of the various stories indicate that this search party, after being shown and finding the bodies of Myrick and Mitchell, buried the remains where they were found there in Monument Valley. It was not until a year or so later, according to Cass Hite, probably in late 1880 or the first half of 1881, that a group of men were sent out by Henry Mitchell to recover the bodies and bring them back for proper burial. Somewhere on the south side of the San Juan River the party was stopped by Navajos under Hashkéneinii. Perhaps exaggerating somewhat, Hite said that the two groups parlayed for some two days before Hashkéneinii finally agreed that Hite and two others of the men could proceed on to get the bodies. Hite concluded by stating that they successfully got the remains, which were then subsequently buried in Montezuma Valley, Colorado.[25]

Bert Loper, close friend and fellow miner of Hite during their later lives in Glen Canyon of the Colorado River in southern Utah, added a significant detail to this story. He stated that Myrick and Mitchell's remains were buried at Mitchell Springs in Montezuma Valley.[26] Mitchell Springs, located today in the far southern part of the town of Cortez, was the site of the ranch and surrounding small settlement of Stanley Mitchell, a brother of Henry Mitchell and uncle of Hernan.

As for the Navajos' Pish-la-ki mine, the story continued to unfold. A contemporary 1880 newspaper article said that Myrick and Mitchell had in their possession very rich quartz ores when their remains were found.[27] In an 1892 article this was echoed when it was stated that several rich specimens of silver were found near the bodies.[28] An 1897 article enlarged upon, and possibly embellished, these accounts.

Perhaps confirming this is the fact that in the 1897 story the silver was now said to be gold. It stated that three sacks of ore were found with the two men, which was later tested in Durango and averaged $450 in gold [sic].[29]

With the much-publicized deaths of the two prospectors, and even more so with the evident discovery of rich silver ore near their bodies, the legend of the Merrick and Mitchell silver mine continued to grow.

Mitchell Butte

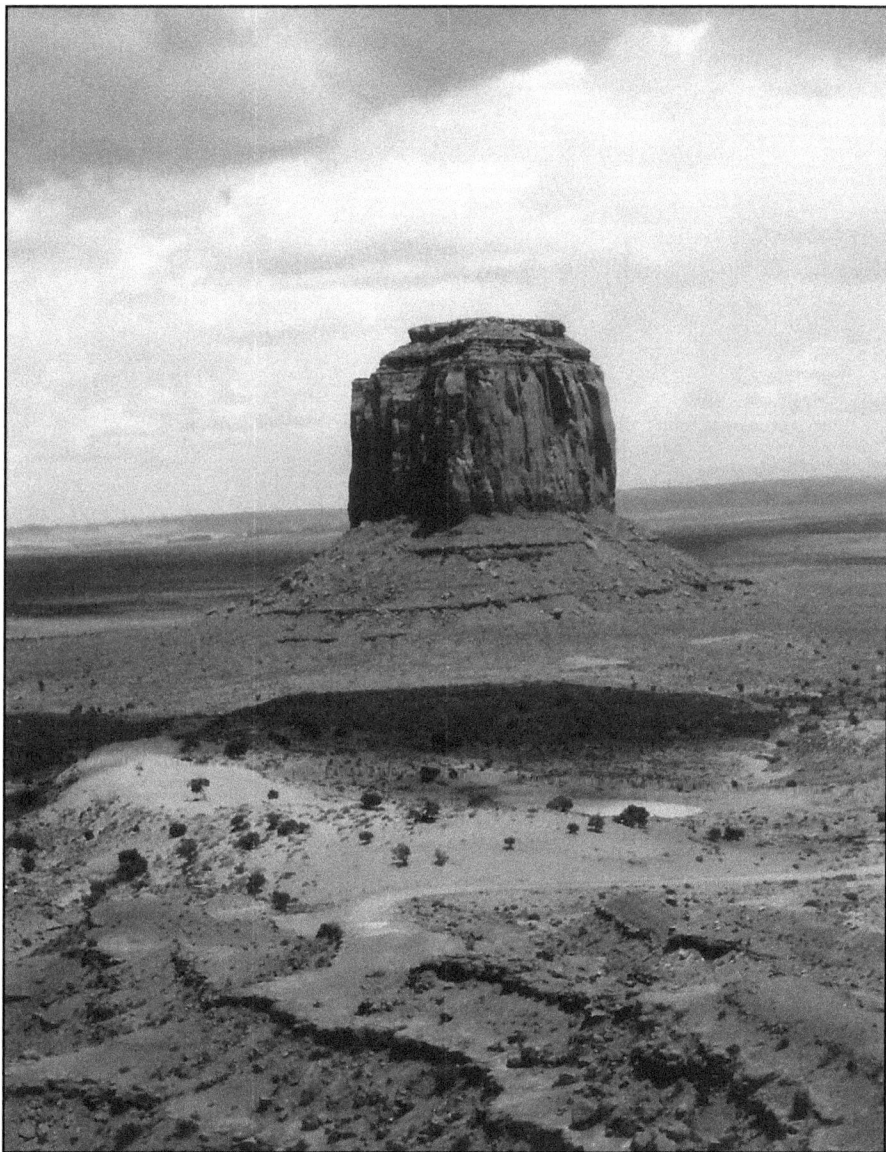

Merrick Butte

Six:

Prospecting Begins

The tragic deaths of Charles Myrick and Hernan Mitchell did nothing to dissuade future prospectors from rushing in to search the countryside around Monument Valley and Navajo Mountain for any trace of the purported silver mine. Indeed, if anything the incident seemed to spur them on in even greater numbers. In the two years following the killings, 1880 and 1881, several hopeful parties entered the northern Navajo region, native opposition notwithstanding.

The first of these parties to follow upon the heels of Myrick and Mitchell started out even before news of their deaths reached the white settlements. On January 10, barely two weeks after the departure of Mitchell and Myrick from the Mitchell ranch, three other prospectors left the mining town of Rico, headed for the new field of excitement at Blue Mountain. They were Patrick "Paddy" Cain, E.D. "Lige" Ledford, and Dave Swickheimer.[1]

Several of the 1880 accounts used the name Blue Mountain for Navajo Mountain. As far back as the 1700s, Spanish explorers had spoken of the *Sierra Azul*, the "Blue Mountains," which lay far to the west of their Rio Grande settlements of New Mexico. On his 1778 map, cartographer Bernardo de Miera showed this Blue Mountain on his map detailing the Dominguez-Escalante expedition of 1776. He located it just south of the junction of what are today the San Juan and Colorado Rivers, confirming that it was, in fact, today's Navajo Mountain. This present name was not bestowed until maps were drawn from the Powell Survey in the early 1870s. From a distance, however, its tree-covered slopes do present a definite bluish-green hue.

Two months later, after the three prospectors had left that mining town, by March 7 so-called "reliable" information was received at the newspaper office that the bodies of Myrick and Mitchell had been found by the latest search party. The group that had started from Rico in early

January had not been heard from and were now absent ten days over their scheduled time to return. It was then feared that this party, which now also was said to include Joe Trimble and Joe Lacombe, had perhaps met a similar fate as had befallen the unfortunate Myrick and Mitchell. The overdue group was said to have been poorly armed and could not have protected themselves very well if they had been the object of an attack.[2]

Three days afterward, however, on the evening of March 10, Dave Swickheimer, Paddy Cain, and Joe Charest, three of the members of the parties which had left Rico, arrived back safe and sound. They reported that the remainder of the party was also safely out of the Navajo country. Joe Lacombe had been left at Mitchell's ranch, Lige Ledford stayed in the Montezuma Valley, while Joe Trimble had gone on to Animas City. They had found some mineral signs, and the three prospectors all believed that there were potentially valuable mines in the area south of Navajo Mountain. They described the country through which the party had traveled as being principally high mesas, separated by deep box canyons and gorges.

Significantly, as far as location is concerned, the three men also declared that west of the mineral section they had found caves cut deep in the solid rock and situated high up in the nearly perpendicular sides of the canyons. In some of these were seen ancient cliff houses. As it was probably at least several centuries since these ruins had been occupied, the shallow steps that had been cut as a means of access had, for the most part, crumbled and washed away.[3]

South of Navajo Mountain, but west of the "mineral section," would have put the prospecting group in today's Navajo Canyon region. There are, in fact, prehistoric cliff dwellings of the Anasazi culture scattered throughout that canyon system, especially in its eastern and northern tributary gorges. One of these is Inscription House Ruin, a unit of the present-day Navajo National Monument.

Later that fall of 1880, a story was picked up from the Animas City *Southwest*, which told of a new proposed expedition into the now celebrated Navajo country. It reportedly was then in the organizational stage at Parrott City, another San Juan Mountain mining town on the La Plata River. The expedition was planned to be made up of some seventy-five men, well-armed, and with sixty days provisions to be taken along.[4]

Shortly after the first of October this expedition, now said to number some eighty-five prospectors, started out on yet another search for the purported silver mine. The party was composed of twenty-five men from Rico, and twenty more from Parrott City and the Mancos Valley. The two congregated at Mitchell's ranch on the San Juan, there to await the arrival of some forty more men from various other locales and mining camps. The three parties were then combined into one large expedition. The party that started from Parrott City and the Mancos Valley was reported to have been in Animas City on Wednesday, October 6, to purchase supplies.[5]

Writing in later years, Louisa Wetherill said that twenty-two men went from the new settlement of Mancos, including her father, John J. "Jack" Wade. They went first to the site of the Myrick and Mitchell killings in Monument Valley but then proceeded to prospect much of the country that lay beyond.[6]

Geologist Herbert E. Gregory, undoubtedly getting his information from Mrs. Wetherill, had earlier given a few more details of this 1880-81 prospecting venture. From the Kayenta region, the expedition had followed the course of Laguna Creek westward to the point where it made an abrupt turn to the north into Tsegi Canyon. In that area Jack Wade described finding small lakes and grassy meadows.[7] These features were not only the source for the name Laguna Creek, but also of the old name for the Tsegi – Laguna, or Lake Canyon. Today the lakes and meadows are gone, drained by the downcutting and arroyo formation of the creek.

Later, Albert H. Spencer stated that in their attempts to find the silver mine, this expedition had traveled as far as Navajo Canyon and its tributary, Segito. Though they did succeed in finding some old smelters, perhaps those originally found by Charles Myrick in 1878 or 1879, they could not locate the actual outcropping of silver.[8] As Louisa Wetherill so descriptively stated, "the mesas and canyons of the Navajo country held their secret well," and the group did not find any clue to the mine. In February of 1881 they returned to Mancos.[9]

Interestingly, a carved inscription found at the site shown on today's U.S. Geological Survey maps as Tse Ya Toe Spring, may be from either the earlier 1880 prospecting party or from this later one. It reads "B. I.

Bill 1880." Tse Ya Toe is the Anglicized spelling of the site's Navajo name and means "Water Under the Rock." This spring, some fifteen miles south of Navajo Mountain, would probably have been a principal watering stop for either expedition. B.I. Bill may have been Benjamin Bill, who was listed as a "laborer" at Keams Canyon, Arizona, in the U.S. census conducted there earlier in June of that year.

In January of 1881, two men named Aaron Stull and Robert Reese came down to the Keams Canyon Trading Post in northern Arizona from the Mitchell settlement. There, Stull was a boarder with Henry Mitchell, and he and Reese had been sent to Keams Canyon to reclaim the mules belonging to Mitchell's son and Charles Myrick. However, before returning to the San Juan, Stull and Reese, at the suggestion of Mr. Mitchell, wanted to make a search for the reported silver mine, this time by approaching the area from the south.

Alexander M. Stephen was at this time in charge of the trading post while Thomas Keam was away on business in Santa Fe, New Mexico. If he would furnish them with needed assistance, Stull and Reese proposed that they, Mr. Mitchell, Stephen, and Mr. Keam, would all share in any profits made from the venture. To this proposal Stephen readily agreed and furnished the two with fresh horses, ample provisions, as well as a Navajo guide. Stull had previously been in the Navajo country, evidently as a member of one or both of the first two searches for Myrick and Mitchell. But he had never been this far south before, and it was necessary for Stephen to furnish them a native guide for the hundred or so miles between Keams Canyon and the area of their proposed exploration.

On the fourth evening out from Keams Canyon, the trio camped on the brink of a canyon that was occupied by Paiutes. Some of the natives came up to visit the camp, and one of them was wearing a cartridge-belt that was recognized by Stull as having belonged to Myrick. As the evening wore on, the Navajo guide reportedly overheard the Paiutes talk of murdering the two Americans. He managed to inform Stull and Reese of the danger, and by careful and prompt actions they were able to make a safe return to Keams Canyon. Subsequently, Stull and Reese then traveled back to the Mitchell ranch with the ransomed mules.[10]

According to a newspaper interview in 1892, John Gavitt (actually the last name should be Gavin) was a member of a little-known, eighteen-man prospecting party which went down into the lower San Juan country in the summer of 1881. They reached the San Juan River by way of one of its tributary streams that came in from the north, about sixty-five miles from its junction with the Colorado River. This was perhaps today's Clay Wash. The group then reportedly followed down the San Juan and prospected as far as the Colorado. However, they met with so much opposition from the local Indians that the prospecting became too dangerous, and the party finally gave up and returned home.[11]

Still another large prospecting party left for the Navajo country in the fall of 1881. Part of the outfit, which consisted of Worden Grigsby, John Clarke, Pat Cain, Jim Hall, Gus Heffernan, S.C. Grant, Lige Ledford, and Mike Murphy, all from Rico, was reportedly preparing to start out in the next few days for Navajo Mountain. There they would search for the storied silver mine of Myrick and Mitchell.[12]

The party left on Wednesday, November 16, and met other groups at Mitchell's San Juan ranch. There they were soon joined by a handful of men from Durango. By the time the entire expedition left the rendezvous, they hoped to have a respectable number of men for safety's sake. They were reportedly well-equipped with fine horses, good guns, and plenty of ammunition and provisions. The stated intention of the expedition was more for the sake of exploring the country and investigating its various resources than with the actual expectation of finding any rich mines. They intended to return about the first of the year (1882).[13]

Longtime prospector Cass Hite was evidently one of the "handful" of men who came from Durango. In the autobiographical poem that he wrote in his later years, he stated that he and four companions had left Durango to go down to the San Juan River and over into the land of the Navajo. There they would hunt for an Indian mine that the natives called the Pish-la-ki.[14] In a letter that Hite wrote to a Denver newspaper in 1893, he provided a few more details. He said that he had entered the Navajo country with a party in the fall of 1881. They had explored that section thoroughly, and many of the names now found on the maps of that region were bestowed at that time by Hite and his fellow prospectors. Significantly, he too said that they explored more than they had time to prospect.[15]

This 1881-82 prospecting party returned to Durango about January 16 from their exploration of the Navajo Mountain area. A local newspaper subsequently interviewed M.S. Foote, a member of the expedition. He reported that the party had gone due west from Durango to the Montezuma Valley, then turned southwest from there to the San Juan River. They then followed that stream west and northwest to Mitchell's ranch at the mouth of the McElmo Creek. Four miles below the ranch the party crossed the San Juan, which at that point flowed in a northwesterly direction. They then traveled west over a rolling plateau region until they struck what the article called Duchesne Canyon. Perhaps the newspaperman misheard, as this was actually what at that time was known as De Chelly Creek – present-day Chinle Wash. The group then crossed what Foote referred to as the Haystack Mountains, undoubtedly today's Comb Ridge, by way of a narrow pass or canyon. A little beyond this, Monumental Valley was reached.

This valley is remarkable for the great number of "monumental" buttes and spires that dot its wide, desert expanse to heights of several hundred feet. Monument Valley today, of course, is known to millions of viewers as the iconic backdrop for many Western movies and seemingly countless television commercials. Foote went on to say that the valley was bounded on the north by the canyon of the San Juan River and on the east and south by the curving and scalloped, upturned sandstone ridge of the Haystack Mountains. To the west it was bounded by an unnamed creek that flowed north to the San Juan. Later that same year this drainage would be christened with its present name of Copper Canyon.

Significantly, Foote said that this creek was lined on its western side by a lengthy rampart of rocky cliffs that rose upward some 1,000 feet. This was the eastern side of what is now called Nokai Mesa. The expedition found this mesa inaccessible for a distance of thirty or forty miles.[16] Though Navajo Mountain, their goal, was not more than a score of miles distant in a straight line to the west, the seemingly impassable mesa forced them to make an extensive detour to the south. It took the party no less than twelve days to finally reach the base of the mountain.

By this time the expedition had been without water for two days, and a search of the general vicinity revealed no sufficient quantity for both men and horses. They then struck off to the southwest and traveled a dozen or so rugged miles before finally finding an ample supply. This direction and distance would have taken them down into the depths of what is today called Forbidding Canyon. There, according to Foote, the men "drank themselves nearly to death" and rested their horses for three days. Present-day Aztec Creek, a perennial stream of clear, flowing water, does in fact course its way through Forbidding Canyon. During their time in what must have seemed like an earthly paradise to them, Foote carved his name and the date on the western wall of the gorge: "M.S. Foote Dec 28th 1881."

After their three-day recuperation, the expedition turned back to Navajo Mountain. There, ironically enough, within a few hundred yards of one of their earlier dry camps, they discovered a living spring of water. This was probably today's Rainbow Lodge Spring, known to later prospectors as Willow Spring. Foote indicated that at this time one full day was spent in exploring Navajo Mountain, and this spring could very well have been found during that search.

During the day-long search, only Foote and one other member of the party actually reached the summit of the mountain. He said that the solitary peak was shaped like a horseshoe opening to the south, an excellent description of where today's Horse Canyon cuts into the southwest flank of the mountain. Off to the east the prospecting duo looked across to a sage and pinyon-dotted plateau expanse, but which was separated from Navajo Mountain by a canyon hundreds of feet in depth. This would be today's Piute Canyon, across which is present-day Piute Mesa. Radiating out on the north was a series of canyons leading toward the San Juan River, which must have been Desha, Cha, and Bald Rock Canyons on modern maps of the area. The expedition then returned to Durango, retracing the same route as they had taken coming in.[17]

Another Durango newspaper also interviewed Foote, and this story was immediately picked up by the Rico tabloid. Here Foote provided additional details about the recent prospecting venture. He said that the party to prospect the country in the vicinity of Navajo Mountain consisted of twenty-five men from Rico and Durango. After they had all assembled at Mitchell's ranch, Aaron Stull was chosen leader of the expedition, as he was the most familiar with that country. This was undoubtedly due to an earlier trip in search of Myrick and Mitchell and his later search for the silver mine from Keams Canyon.

From the San Juan the party traveled over what Foote called the old Moencopi [sic] trail southwest to the mouth of Lake Canyon, today's Tsegi Canyon in northern Arizona. This would have been the lengthy "detour" mentioned in the previous newspaper article. They then followed Lake Canyon north. This portion of the trip through present-day Tsegi Canyon is confirmed by an inscription that Foote left carved into that gorge's sandstone wall near Peach Spring. It is his name and the date, "M.S. Foote Dec 16 1881."

The expedition traveled some twenty-five miles from the mouth of Foote's Lake Canyon to Navajo Mountain. They probably exited the gorge and climbed up onto the level plateau to the northwest by way of today's Bubbling Spring Canyon. This tributary opens into the Tsegi almost straight across from Peach Spring and the Foote inscription. Even today a Navajo trail exists here, leading up and then out of Bubbling Spring Canyon.

Navajo Mountain is the only peak rising above the plateau level for scores of miles in all directions. Here Foote added an important detail about their day's exploration of the mountain. He stated that examination of its exposed rock outcroppings proved them to be only sandstone. The prevailing sentiment of most mining men of the time was that precious metals such as gold and silver were to only be found as lode deposits in igneous, or volcanic rock, not sedimentary such as sandstone.

The expedition's lack of water was exacerbated because there was no snow in the country, except for a little on Navajo Mountain itself. When their provisions began to run low, it was finally decided to return home. Significantly, for later expeditions, Foote concluded by saying that they had seen only three Paiutes and were well treated by all of the Navajos they met.

Though no valuable mineral had been discovered, the ever-hopeful prospectors were still not discouraged.[18] This party believed that the silver lode discovered by Myrick and Mitchell was located in one of the canyons between Monumental Valley and Navajo Mountain. However, so far as that objective was concerned, the prospectors were unsuccessful.[19]

Inscription House Ruin

Tsegi Canyon

B.I. Bill, 1880
Tse Ya Toe Spring

Aztec Creek
Forbidding Canyon

Seven:

The Foote Expedition

M.S. Foote, in actual occupation, was the Durango agent for the Pioneer Stage Line. He is a prime example of the types of men who joined the various prospecting parties in search of the Myrick and Mitchell silver mine. These were not only made up of career mining men and veteran prospectors, but also included townspeople of all businesses and trades, as well as cattlemen and farmers. But all held dear to their hearts the fervent hope of "striking it rich."

It was probably no coincidence that the Durango newspapers interviewed Foote when the latest prospecting party returned to Durango in mid-January of 1882. Within the week still another group was already forming to return once again to the Navajo Mountain country, and elected as its "Captain" was M.S. Foote.[1]

On January 24 the *Durango Record* listed the names of twenty-four men who were members of what may be termed the Foote Expedition. They were M.S. Foote, G.W. Seaman, Joe Duckett, Louis Keyes, Ben Rice, A.D. Donley, Cash Cade, Frank Winchell, Chas Beatty, Levi Morelander, G.P. Foster, George Emmerson, George Miller, Samuel McLane, Cass Hite, Ed Gross, Robert Glazier, John Pollax, N.C. Young, John Breichao, C.W. Weihl, J.C. Wileman, Eb O'Dell, and partner.

With the exception of eight or nine men, this party started out from Durango on January 23rd. That evening Foote himself traveled southwest the few miles to the U.S. military post of Fort Lewis, as he had been requested to come there on his way out of town by General George P. Buell, the commanding officer. The general evidently wished to obtain whatever information he could in regard to the Indian situation in the area that had been visited by the earlier prospecting party. Afterward, Foote and the remaining eight or nine men left Durango the following day.[2]

Letters were received by the *Record* shortly before February 8 that told of the early progress of the expedition. The first, dated February 1 from Mitchell's Ranch, said that nothing of importance had occurred up to that point. However, it had been a very hard trip to the San Juan and had "snowed like hell" all the way. They would start out from Mitchell's the next day. The letter was signed T.B. Reed.[3]

The second letter was posted from "Mormon Cabins, Near McElmo," on February 2. This place was very likely the Mormon settlement more commonly known as Fort Montezuma, just a few miles west of the Mitchell enclave and the mouth of McElmo Wash. This writer stated that the number of men leaving the next day for Navajo Mountain was thirty-five. Evidently several additional members had been added to those who had originally departed from Durango.[4] The author of this letter signed his name simply "Mac." This may have been Samuel McLane, but the wording of the letter, the tone used, and its tongue-in-cheek statements, all suggest that it was actually Cass Hite who penned the letter.

As for the subsequent journey of the expedition, very little was written about it in any of the contemporary newspapers. This was undoubtedly due to the fact that this exploration of the Navajo Mountain region unfortunately did not amount to as much as was hopefully expected. Evidently this party held to the prevailing belief of the previous one as to the probable location of the now seemingly lost silver mine. But though they prospected every canyon from the mouth of today's Chinle Wash west to Navajo Mountain, they were unsuccessful in finding anything of value in the mineral line.[5]

The general route taken to Navajo Mountain ultimately followed that of the previous expedition. However, led by Foote, the present party must have once again attempted to travel directly west from Monument Valley to Navajo Mountain. Evidently this time they were able to surmount the eastern cliffs of Nokai Mesa, but were then seemingly stymied by the depths of today's Nokai Canyon beyond. It was later stated that when within a dozen miles of the mountain, the party had to return to Monument Valley to get around a deep canyon.[6] Soon afterward, this obstacle began to be known as Foote Canyon.[7]

Back in Monument Valley once more, the expedition trekked south and west to the mouth of Tsegi Canyon, circumventing the high mesas and deep canyons to the west and north. Once again taking advantage of the open mouth of the Tsegi, they followed up that gorge and then across the intervening plateau to Navajo Mountain. This is known from the presence of several historic inscriptions, which can still be seen today, that different members of the expedition left in the sandstone rock at various locations along this line of march.

The first of these are on a low canyon wall just south of Peach Spring, obviously a regular watering stop for both Native American Indians and American prospectors. Perhaps taking a cue from M.S. Foote who had left his name and the date at the same location in December of 1881, two of the present prospectors carved their names close by. One is the name "J.A. Duckett," while the other is the initials "G. E." This last is undoubtedly those of George Emmerson.

Once up and out of the Tsegi and Bubbling Spring Canyon, the expedition would have passed Tse Ya Toe Spring on the rolling and sometimes hill-studded plateau that led north to Navajo Mountain. Though the previous prospecting party, suffering from a lack of water, had evidently missed this water source – admittedly a quarter-mile or so off the trail to the west – the present party did not. Close to the "B. I. Bill" inscription from 1880, present expedition member George Miller added his initials and last name: "G.M. Miller."

From Navajo Mountain, or perhaps even before they reached that point, the expedition turned abruptly off to the west and evidently followed a still-existing Navajo trail down into the depths of the upper reaches of today's Navajo Canyon. To the native Navajo the area of these upper gorges was known collectively as *Nii tsí'ii*, though on modern maps just one individual branch is shown as Nitsin Canyon, the English spelling of the *Diné* name. This seems to have been the same locale that was visited by the first prospecting party from Rico two years earlier. Whether the present expedition was aware of this is not known.

That the 1882 party was, in fact, at Nitsin is again documented by inscriptions left in the area. On the north side of Nitsin Canyon, on the wall of a small cave at the left side of the alcove housing the prehistoric cliff dwelling of Inscription House Ruin, is carved "C.M. Cade A.D. 1882." Nearby is written, in what was probably wet charcoal, "N.C. Young 1882." Just to the north, across a low saddle in the intervening plateau wall, is another headward branch of Navajo Canyon – Toenleshushe. This is the Americanized spelling of the Navajo name meaning "boiling" or "bubbling water," and refers to water welling up in a flowing spring.

On the north side of Toenleshushe Canyon is a rather small, unimposing Anasazi ruin known today as The Fortress. On the side wall of its sheltering alcove, and again written in either charcoal or the burnt end of a stick, is once more written the name of "N.C. Young." This time, however, it is dated, "Mar. 6, 1882." Lastly, just north of the mouth of Toenleshushe Canyon, high on the eastern side of Navajo Creek, is carved the name of "J.A. Duckett." Joe Duckett had incised his name back in Tsegi Canyon near Peach Spring, but with no date. Here, however, he conveniently added "Mar. 6, 1882."

At this point the expedition seems to have temporarily split up. Once more this is indicated by inscriptions left by members of the party. On March 8, M.S. Foote left his name and that date carved on the side of a prominent butte some thirty-five miles to the northwest, overlooking the drainage of today's West Canyon Creek. These miles are across some extremely rugged canyon country, and it would have been nearly impossible that all of the men of the party could have reached this point by March 8, just two short days after the March 6 inscriptions back in the Nitsin area. Most likely, Foote and just a handful of companions took off on this side venture to the northwest, while the main body of the expedition remained at the well-watered and grass-covered Nitsin locale.

On Foote's earlier trip to the Navajo Mountain country, when he and a companion climbed to its very summit, from that high vantage point they had carefully examined the surrounding jumble of sandstone canyons with a critical eye. It was probably then that Foote discerned that the drainage of West Canyon Creek led northwest all the way to the Colorado River. From the inscription butte it was just one day's ride down the wide, sandy swath of the south fork of the canyon – what the Navajos call *Séí Bii'bikoh*, "Sand Canyon" – to the Colorado. In a later newspaper article, it was stated that the only place in which the expedition found anything of mineral value was in the bed of the Colorado River.[8] Based on the location of Foote's March 8 inscription, the mouth of West Canyon Creek must have been that place.

The prospectors obviously recognized that the Colorado during this winter season was extremely low, and realized that the placer gold deposits they discovered there would be underwater for most of the year following the annual spring rise of the river. Foote and his small party, therefore, spent but one day test-panning along the bank of the river. This is yet again shown by the presence of a second name and date back on the small, but prominent, inscription butte. This one reads, "M. Murphy Mar. 10, 1882," and was evidently inscribed on their return trip by expedition member Mike Murphy.

Foote and his exploring party reunited with the main group back at Nitsin, and then climbed back out of the depths of Navajo Canyon and up onto the plateau above. At this juncture they were some fifteen miles south of Navajo Mountain. Here it was found that they now had an insufficient supply of provisions to sustain the entire expedition for the time required for them to enter a small section of country which they had not yet explored. Therefore, a major split resulted. Eight of the men started directly back to Colorado, while sixteen others remained in the Navajo country to continue the search for the elusive silver mine. Five of these sixteen, however, including M.S. Foote, wended their way southward toward the Moqui (Hopi) Indian villages and the U.S. Indian Agency located at Keams Canyon.[9]

These men had heard it said that the Indians had taken to this agency the original wooden stakes of the Myrick-Mitchell mine. Therefore, they wanted to visit the agency to find out the facts of the matter. On arrival they were advised by Thomas Keam, who was not only the local trader but also the government Indian agent, that the stakes were actually nothing more than survey markers from the 1870s' U.S. government Wheeler Survey. Keam also said that for some time he had been making offers of various goods to the Indians if they would bring to him samples of the purported silver ore from the Myrick-Mitchell mine, but to no avail. Ore that had been brought in, and which the Indians claimed to contain "pish-la-ki," or silver, proved to be of no value when tested.[10]

The party of prospectors that had started directly back to Colorado, as well as those from Keams Canyon, both arrived in Durango by March 30. Those that were listed in a subsequent newspaper article were S.H. McLane, George Seaman, M.S. Foote, Lewis Keyes, Arthur Ames, Eb.

O'Dell, Charles Beatty, Lewis Moorlander, Alexander Darby, and David Castleman.[11]

The prospectors who had remained behind to look further for the hidden silver of Navajo Mountain returned just shortly before April 14. Those named were William Ross, Charles Niche, William Goin, Harry Hope, Notley Young, Lorenzo Reed, Cass Hite, Cash Cade, Gus Heffernan, and John Wall.[12] Because of carved inscriptions that were left behind, two other members of this third party must have been George Miller and George Emmerson.

From the separation point of the three groups, this remaining third party had headed back north to Navajo Mountain. Already knowing of the water source at Tse Ya Toe, George Miller for a second time left his name on the wall of the sheltering alcove. Once at Navajo Mountain, they turned to the southwest and made their way down into present-day Forbidding Canyon. The party probably descended by way of a Navajo trail that reaches Aztec Creek not far downstream from the point where M.S. Foote had left his name and the date back in December of 1881. Within just a few feet of this earlier inscription, George Emmerson now incised "Geo. Emmerson 1882."

Forbidding Canyon must have been the small section of country that had not yet been explored. The earlier expedition, though they had stayed there for three days, had most likely not searched to any extent in either direction. Perhaps the present party wanted to follow Aztec Creek to the north where it, like West Canyon Creek, flows into the Colorado River. Possibly they hoped that placer gold could be found there as well. What they could not have known, but undoubtedly quickly discovered, was that just a few miles downcanyon the creek poured over steep drop-offs which are impassable to horses and other pack stock.

By the first of April, this party was back up at the foot of Navajo Mountain. On the line of white sandstone cliffs that tower just above today's Rainbow Lodge Spring, George Emmerson once again left his name, this time with the date: "Geo. Emmerson Ap. 1 1882." This was probably the same spring of water that had been discovered the preceding winter.

Upon finally getting back to Durango, this third and last group gave a much more satisfactory and promising account than the earlier ones had expressed. While these men had admittedly seen nothing of the fabled Myrick-Mitchell mine itself, they did exhibit large buttons of what appeared to be silver ore from crude smelters they had found in Tsegi Canyon. They believed that if the Indians were able to get such results by their crude smelting methods, then professional miners should be able to obtain even more lucrative returns. Finally, and perhaps most importantly, they had also discovered what they said was a "large ledge of silver-bearing ore," and had mineral specimens to prove it.[13]

Across Nokai Canyon to Nokai Mesa

Peach Spring area
Tsegi Canyon

Navajo Mountain
From Tse Ya Toe Spring

M.S. Foote, Mar. 8th 1882
Above West Canyon Creek

Eight:

The Cass Hite Searches

Cass Hite was born in 1845 in Illinois. It was in 1866, after the Civil War, that he first went west to try his hand at prospecting and mining, on this occasion in Montana and Idaho. For the next fifteen years he followed mineral strikes from mining camp to mining camp including Mexico, Arizona, and eventually Colorado. There, at Rico, Hite had his first encounter with the story of the Pish-la-ki silver mine. As detailed previously, for the next three years he was a part of several expeditions in search of the fabled lode. From his own writings and interviews with various newspapers, as well as a published book by a nationally-known author in 1898, Cass Hite has become one of the best known and most recognizable participants in the quest for the Lost Myrick and Mitchell Silver Mine.[1]

In the spring of 1882, a report was received in Durango that must have had a stunning effect on all of the folk who either knew of, or had looked for, the long-sought mine – the great Myrick-Mitchell mine had at last been found. The fortunate discoverer was none other than Cass Hite, one of the members of the Foote expedition which had left Durango a few weeks earlier for Navajo Mountain. This report was made by Major W.H. Rowe, who had just returned from surveying the Southern Ute Indian Reservation. Yes, the Myrick and Mitchell mine had been discovered, but however, what Hite failed to mention, and was very likely intentional on his part, was that it was not the storied silver mine of the Navajos.[2]

One of the basic objectives of ancient alchemy was the transmutation of base metals into gold. And this, in an allegorical sense, is what happened to the recently reported "large ledge of silver-bearing ore." This important fact was eventually brought out a few weeks later in an article in one of the Durango newspapers. On May 17, the latest and best equipped party of prospectors which had yet gone into that region left for the Monument Valley country. The object of this expedition was to take possession of what was now referred to as a "great copper mine," no longer silver, which had been discovered the past March by Cass Hite on his last exploring trip. The article declared that this huge find should be named the Cass Hite Lode, but Hite himself objected and stated that in commemoration of his fallen predecessors, the vein should be called the Myrick and Mitchell Lode.[3]

Though this latest expedition was at times referred to as an exploring party, in actuality it was not even a prospecting party. It was a group of miners returning to an already located claim with the intent of performing all the further requirements of mining law and beginning actual extraction of the copper itself. The following members were named and were said to have all been through the Monumental Valley and Navajo Mountain country at least once and some twice: Cass Hite, a mining prospector of many years' experience; Joseph A. Duckett, trail hunter; George M. Miller and James E. Porter, prospectors. The names of three others were not known at the time.[4]

Hite was likely the nominal leader of this venture. Officially he was elected "recorder" of the expedition,[5] a recorder being in a sense a secretary. To this person fell the responsibilities of keeping track of all proceedings, the recording (thus the title) of locations and claims with the proper authorities, and, just as importantly, the boosting of opportunities for possible investors in the mining scheme. In this latter regard, Hite was to keep the various town newspapers apprised of all goings on and happenings – at least those of a positive nature.

The new mining area was formally named the Capitán Mining District, after the towering, black, volcanic neck marking the southern boundary of Monument Valley and which the prospectors had dubbed the Copper Capitán. This is what is now shown as Agathla Peak on present-day maps. The claim itself was located in what the miners called Copper Canyon, a name it still retains today.[6]

In a letter to the editor dated October 25, 1882, Hite gave the location of the Copper Canyon mines as twelve or fifteen miles south of the San Juan River, east of Navajo Mountain, and very near the line running between the territories of Arizona and Utah. In which territory they actually were situated was not positively known, but the probability was that they were in Arizona. However, the new mining district embraced claims in both territories.[7]

The formal bounds of the Capitán Mining District were described as commencing at the mouth of the Rio de Chilli, or De Shay (present-day Chinle Wash), and running westerly along the course of the San Juan River to its confluence with the Colorado; then down the Colorado River to the mouth of West Canyon (today's Navajo Canyon); then up West Canyon to the northern base of White Mesa, and due east to the boundary of the Navajo Indian Reservation. Finally, then, the line ran north to the place of beginning.[8] These bounds would have included both Monument Valley and Navajo Mountain.

Hite also answered what were evidently persistent inquiries about the reputed Myrick-Mitchell silver mine. He said that whether any such mine actually existed, they did not know, but certainly they had not found it. Hite added, however, that the Navajo did profess to have a silver mine known as Pish-la-ki, and further, that if any *Diné* revealed its location, he was threatened with death.[9]

Evidently the copper deposits in Copper Canyon did not live up to their supposed potential. And perhaps they were never intended to do so. It is entirely conceivable that the touting of the sure-fire copper prospects was purposely meant to be safer, and therefore more enticing to possible investors, than the more dangerous and unsure search for the Navajo's Pish-la-ki mine. But financial backing for the location of the Myrick-Mitchell silver may have actually been the miners' real, but disguised, intent all along. By the fall of 1882, Cass Hite at least was hot on that trail. This was clearly shown by an incident near the end of an entirely separate prospecting expedition, this one from the Mancos Valley area.

In the winter of 1882-83 a party of eight, consisting of Jack Wade, Jim Kevelin, Bill Clemens, Carl Scharnhorst, Jim Barnes, Gus Honaker, Nathan Kilburn, and James M. Rush, Jr., set out to look for the Myrick and Mitchell mine. Another separate party of five also set out at the same time. They were Joe Moore, Bill Reid, Billy Thatcher, and two others.

According to Rush, in an interview years later, both parties made their way to the little Mormon town of Bluff, crossed the San Juan River, went down to Willow Springs and then over to Tsegi Canyon. They then climbed up onto the mesa west of the canyon, today's Tall Mountain area, and made their way around the head of Piute Canyon. At this point, during the night, Indians ran off some of the first party's horses and demanded money to get them back. The next night the prospectors were sitting around the fire when the Indians this time stampeded all of their horses and burros. Fortunately, the second prospecting party was camped not far down the valley from the first, and they ran ahead of the fleeing stock and were able stop them. The first party of eight, which included Rush, stayed in that camp for three more days before they finally decided to return home.

Rush now stated that on the way back they came upon a white man living in Monument Valley among the Navajos, and who was attempting to find out where the Myrick-Mitchell mine was located. This was evidently Cass Hite. Seeming to confirm this is the fact that the man then showed them where Hernan Mitchell had been buried and also directed them to the base of the monument by which Charles Myrick had been buried.[10] Hite would have known both of these locations from his being a part of the party which had gone in to recover the bodies a year or so earlier.

By early spring of 1883, it was reported that a Colonel Bowen had taken a bond on the Gold Hill Mine, situated in Moonlight Canyon. This was the drainage immediately to the east of Copper Canyon, known today by the Americanized version of its Navajo name – Oljeto. Significantly, it was also stated that the original owners of the copper property had now gone to Lake and East Canyons, present-day Tsegi and Piute Canyons, in search of the "wonderful Myrick and Mitchell silver mine."[11]

The last that is heard of this venture came from Hyde's Ferry on the San Juan River, the Mormon's Fort Montezuma, at the end of May. Writing under the pseudonym of "Copper," Cass Hite optimistically reported that they had, in fact, discovered some rich mines. In particular they had found some black ore which they believed were sulphides of silver. They believed they had struck the same belt of black leads which Myrick had, and from which he had obtained his valuable ore. Hite also declared that they had come upon signs of Myrick's actual campfire and indications of work he had done back in 1879. The black leads were capped with sandstone, which up until then had fooled all earlier prospectors except Myrick.[12]

Interestingly, this account by Hite seems to have been confirmed later in the 1950s by Arthur H. Spencer. Spencer stated unequivocally that the lost silver mine was located near the heads of Nokai and Copper Canyons. He described an old Native American trail that led from Hoskaninni Mesa and crossed the heads of the two canyons. Reportedly getting his information from Hashkéneinii Biyé sometime in the 1920s, Spencer said that this was the trail that Myrick and Mitchell had last traveled before their deaths. He also added the key point that the site was one day's ride from Monument Valley. Spencer went on to say that the heads of Nokai and Copper Canyons were caused by faults and that the silver ore had been thrust up through one of them. However, he did concede that there were several faults in that area, and since he was on foot at the time and the country was so rough and broken up, he could not travel to examine all of them.[13]

The 1883 letter of Cass Hite also contained one very significant piece of information – the continual presence of Hashkéneinii. All of the subsequent accounts that eventually appeared concerning Hite are second-hand, but each place the Navajo leader in an important and pivotal role.

A decade later, in 1893, two of Hite's brothers, who were at that time working with him in Glen Canyon in south-central Utah, related the following story to a traveling newspaper correspondent. In the early 1880s, Hite had begun to cultivate the acquaintance of Hashkéneinii, and soon learned from him that the Navajo did indeed have a mine they called Pish-la-ki. Here native silver had been deposited ages past on a rock shelf. Hite also found out that the Indians had by now quarried all of the silver that was in sight and easily broken off, and therefore the mine was, at this time, available for purchase. In time an agreement was reached, and Hashkéneinii was to show the mine to Hite for 2,000 silver dollars. However, a strong sentiment quickly arose among the rest of the band of *Diné* against any such sale of the mine. Ultimately, Hite had to finally abandon his scheme and soon left the land of the Navajo.[14]

In the early 1900s, after Hite had established himself as a placer gold miner along the Colorado River in south-central Utah, fellow miner Bert Loper related the following version of the tale. In the fall of 1882, Hite left Copper Canyon and went and spent the winter at Hashkéneinii's camp. The Navajo leader evidently took a fancy to him and even made him his blood brother. According to Hite, via Loper, in the spring of 1883 he thought the time was finally ripe to begin working on Hashkéneinii about their Pish-la-ki silver mine. However, he had to proceed slowly and cautiously, and it was late summer before he finally got him to agree to sell the mine for 2,000 silver dollars. But the rest of Hashkéneinii's band soon began to distrust Hite's motives. A council was ultimately called to decide the matter, and the prevailing feeling proved to be very much against sale of the mine. That night Hashkéneinii came and woke Hite. His people did not trust him and were becoming more and more hostile. Therefore, he could not show him the mine. Hite then quickly left the camp and departed the area.[15]

In Hashkéneinii Biyé's 1939 interview, he provided a first-hand account of these events and, perhaps even more importantly, from the Navajo point of view. He said that in 1881 [sic] a white man, Cass Hite, had come alone into the Navajo country. He rode into Hashkéneinii's camp and asked for something to eat. The Navajos gave him some meat and, since he was now their guest, according to *Diné* custom they could not do him any harm. He then proceeded to stay with them all summer and became a good friend.

Hite had some pieces of ore with him asked the Navajos if they had seen any rock like it anywhere in the surrounding region. They did not understand different metals, except silver, but Hashkéneinii refused to tell Hite where to find the Pish-la-ki mine. He stayed with the Navajos for three months and picked up many different kinds of rocks. Hashkéneinii Biyé said that he rode with him all over the country, but they never found any valuable minerals. Hite finally gave up and eventually left the Navajo camp.

The next time that Hashkéneinii Biyé encountered Hite was in Copper Canyon the following year, 1882. He saw horse tracks, followed them, and came upon Hite collecting samples of mineral ore. According to the Navajo, Hite came back to their country yet again in 1883, and it was at this time that he finally went down White Canyon to the Colorado River and found placer gold in the sands of that stream.[16]

But though there are a handful of inconsistencies and contradictions in these three accounts, for being given well after the fact they are all in agreement as to the general sequence of events. Hashkéneinii Biyé's date of 1881 for Hite's lengthy stay at the Navajo encampment is probably one year too early, but this lapse in memory may not be surprising after the passage of over fifty years. The biggest difference between the two white men stories and the Native American account seems to be the dramatic rendition of Hashkéneinii's agreement to sell the Pish-la-ki mine, the tense and eventually dangerous council with Hashkéneinii's band, and the subsequent protection of Hite by his Navajo friend. These are in all probability embellishments added to the story by Hite, his relatives, and perhaps even the newspaper correspondent in 1893 who eventually published the account. Hite himself, in 1889, only tersely stated: "For this mine we hunted and took many chances.... It became a little too ticklish for me and I abandoned the hunt."[17]

A few years later, in 1893, Hite reportedly told prospector James W. Black a story that was very down-to-earth and without any sort of exciting encounters that would have put himself in a more favorable light. Hite said that he had been to the Navajo Mountain region back in the 1880s while seeking the Myrick-Mitchell silver mine. After a time, Hashkéneinii finally agreed to take him to the prospect. However, after being provided with supplies and some money, Hashkéneinii only wandered around for five or six weeks, until Hite finally gave up the search. He ultimately realized that Hashkéneinii either did not actually know the location of the mine, or was just stringing him along for whatever he could get in the way of goods and payment.[18]

This account has the ring of truth to it and could very well have been an accurate telling of the true facts of the matter. Hashkéneinii Biyé himself said that his father had early on decided to never show the Pish-la-ki mine to any *bilagáána*, or white man. Indeed, only six other "elders" of his band knew the actual location of the silver. Hashkéneinii realized only too well what would inevitably happen if the mine was opened to white exploitation – the Navajo would undoubtedly soon lose their homeland and be forced elsewhere. Therefore, close friend or not,

Hite was not going to be shown the source of silver. And any other white prospectors would either be led astray, or even killed.

Sometime in the 1930s a story was told by Henry Chee Dodge which seems to back up and give at least some credence to the above account and supposition. Dodge was the son of a white father and Navajo mother. In the early 1880s he became the official Navajo interpreter to the U.S. military, and in 1883 was appointed head of the newly formed Navajo Tribal Police.

According to Dodge, after it came to the attention of the U.S. Indian Agent at Fort Defiance that at least some of the prospectors who had gone to search for gold and silver in the Navajo country had been killed, he sent him to go and learn the true facts of the matter. Dodge then went out and stayed with various Navajo friends for a lengthy amount of time. Whenever a healing ceremony or other type of gathering was held, he attended. He often saw white men's clothes and guns exchange hands in gambling games or at horseraces, and always the story of where the goods came from led back to Hashkéneinii. When a prospector would disappear, his horses and equipment eventually found their way to the camp of Hashkéneinii.

White traders also came to Fort Defiance and claimed that Hashkéneinii had defrauded them. He would agree to bring them rich gold or silver ore if they would first give him food and other supplies to go out and get the precious metal. They gave him the goods he wanted, but would never get any gold or silver in return. Finally, when Hashkéneinii could fool no more traders, he began to hang around the railroad towns, or send some of his band to show samples of rich ore to eager, and gullible, Easterners. The newcomers would then equip themselves for a long stay away from civilization and slip out into the Indian country following a native guide. However, they would then be led into a trap. A few weeks later Hashkéneinii or some of his clansmen would be found innocently hanging around town once again.

Consequently, Dodge formed a plan. He got word to Hashkéneinii that he wished to obtain a share of the silver that he owned. Hashkéneinii eventually sent reply back to bring a pack train and meet him out in the plateau country, where he would then take Dodge to the mine. However, instead of a pack train, Dodge took along ten soldiers and arrived a week earlier than the agreed upon date. The soldiers hid themselves, and he went into the camp alone. Hashkéneinii was not pleased to see him and kept stalling about where the silver was located.

Finally, Dodge challenged Hashkéneinii and said that he did not speak the truth, and his story of silver was a lie. He knew of no silver mine in Monument Valley or Navajo Mountain, and the rich ore that he would show around had actually come from a white man's mine up north. According to this story of Dodge's, Hashkéneinii finally admitted that his ore samples in fact had come from the San Juan Mountains in Colorado.[19]

Whether all of this was true or not, the general implication in the story is probably accurate. Hashkéneinii very well could have led gullible prospectors and others astray, making sure that they never got too close to the actual Pish-la-ki mine, and getting whatever he could from them in the way of money or provisions in the bargain. Future accounts would seem to confirm this.

Cass Hite, at any rate, by now had certainly had his fill of fruitless searches for the legendary silver mine. From this time on it was the lure of lustrous gold that would fulfill the remainder of his life.

Cass Hite, Late 1880's
Utah State Historical Society

Copper Canyon area

Head of Nokai Canyon

Haskéneinii Biyé, 1909
Courtesy of Harvey Leake, Wetherill Collection

Nine:

The Dream Continues

The first large prospecting party, that of 1881-82, had seen only three Paiutes and had been well-treated by all the Navajos they encountered. They even reported the natives as friendly and willing to trade, and that the Navajos in particular provided them with corn to feed the prospectors' horses. The Foote expedition, however, related that while not being bothered in any serious way, the Indians they did meet acted in a very belligerent manner. This second group believed that if their party had not been as large as it was, they may not have fared as well as they fortunately did.

This changing behavior on the part of the natives residing in the Navajo Mountain area should not come as any surprise. It was merely indicative of the old saying, "Fool me once, shame on you. Fool me twice, shame on me." The initial prospecting expedition had met with seeming acceptance and even friendliness. However, with the almost immediate coming of the second, even larger party, these feelings quickly changed to ones of distrust and suspicion. It seemed to be yet another example of the foreign, white people wanting to intrude upon and exploit what belonged to, and was located on, Native American soil.

With the collapse of the Copper Canyon bubble in 1883, the days of large, well-equipped expeditions into the Navajo country for the most part came to an end. For the next two decades any continued searches for the silver of the Myrick and Mitchell mine were usually conducted by either brave, or perhaps foolhardy, individuals and small parties numbering but a handful of prospectors. An example of this was Philip Zoeller, formerly a farmer near Pueblo, Colorado.

Soon after 1880, undoubtedly as a result of the media attention given the deaths of Myrick and Mitchell and their now well-publicized search for the silver of the Pish-la-ki mine, Zoeller first made his way to northern Arizona and the Navajo country. At Keams Canyon he said that "his party separated," and since that place was closer to the locality he wanted to prospect, he remained there working at Thomas Keam's trading post.[1] On March 10, 1882, Zoeller outfitted at Keam's and was supplied with provisions and a Navajo guide. The two made a journey as far north as Navajo Mountain, but eventually returned and reported that they had been unable to find any mineral.[2]

At the first of May, 1882, James R. Sutherland, clerk of the Navajo Agency at Fort Defiance, reported that prospector J.P. Williams had informed him that he had recently traveled directly through the Navajo country and all the way to Navajo Mountain.[3]

Jonathan P. Williams, a native of California, had come with his family to northern Arizona sometime after 1880 to try and find a lost mine a friend of his had told him about. This mine was supposedly located on, or near, Navajo Mountain. He first opened a small trading store at Fort Defiance, but in 1882 eventually moved farther west to Blue Canyon to be nearer Navajo Mountain and the lost mine that he was seeking.[4] Significantly, it was prospector William A. Ross who told Williams about the property at Blue Canyon.[5]

According to a brief item in the Rico newspaper, sometime before June 3, 1882, William Ross and his party had left for the Navajo country. By that date, however, apprehension had begun to grow in regard to their safety and exact whereabouts.[6] Their location was answered, at least partially, in a statement later given in August to U.S. Indian Agent Galen Eastman at Fort Defiance. Ross said that he had been prospecting for the last few months in the country lying to the northwest of the fort.[7]

During this same time period, Eastman had sent his brother, Edward N. Eastman, and his Navajo Interpreter, Henry Chee Dodge, on a mission to locate Haskéneinii's band and establish friendly relations with them. Either accompanying these men from Fort Defiance, or at least returning with them from the Navajo country, were prospectors William Ross and Jonathan P. Williams. Like Ross, Williams stated that for the last few months he had been prospecting far to the northwest.[8]

Eastman's contingent did, in fact, locate Hashkéneinii and his band, but exactly where is not stated. The encounter could have taken place either in the Monument Valley or Navajo Mountain areas. It is known for a fact, however, that during the summer months Williams was near Navajo Mountain. Just to the southwest, in the upper part of Forbidding Canyon, he left his carved name, J. P. Williams, and the date of June 2, 1882. Several miles away, in an eastern tributary of Aztec Creek, is once again found his name, this time with a date of July 4, 1882. Finally, Williams' name is also found twice at Tse Ya Toe Spring, probably indicating stops there on his way in to Navajo Mountain, and then once again on his way back out.

Navajo Mountain must have been literally crowded with hopeful prospectors during the spring and summer of the following year, 1883. Cass Hite, writing from Copper Canyon, said that Mr. Blair Burwell, the assayer, and Mr. Mague, the lawyer, were making an extensive and exhaustive search around the Navajo Mountain. However, they had not been heard from for a month and were now overdue. Doc Christian and Charlie Thomas had gone to the forbidden ground at the head of Lake (Tsegi) Canyon and were also now overdue. Finally, Cash Cade, Cyrus Beard, Joe Duckett, George M. Miller, and James Porter, each of them prominent owners in the Copper Canyon mines, were all absent on different searches for the Myrick-Mitchell mine.[9]

William A. Ross, prospecting partner of J.P. Williams, was also still in the Navajo country in 1883. Yet another newspaper article by the prolific Cass Hite reported that one man now on the trail of the Pish-la-ki mine was a former Durango resident who had once owned a half-interest in a good business on First Street. Hite said that this man had spent a considerable amount of time and money the previous year among the Navajos and was once again back with them. Though he was now said to be broke, they seemed to regard him as a good fellow and thought as much of him as ever. Haskéneinii had even adopted him and promised to show his new *bilagáana* son the fabled Pish-la-ki after a specified time, according to Indian custom, of acceptable behavior.

Hite went on to say that he and his party had seen this "former paleface" several days earlier along with seven other Indians. He had told Hite's group in no uncertain terms that they were on forbidden ground, sacred soil, and insisted that they return at once across the San Juan River. To this demand Hite's party refused, but they did leave the immediate area. Hite concluded by stating that this gentleman evidently had a good racket going and ought to succeed.[10]

That this "former Durangoite" was in fact William Ross was confirmed just two weeks later. George W. Spencer had arrived in Durango from the San Juan on the morning of May 18 and immediately announced that the long sought Pish-la-ki mine had been discovered. This news had been brought to Mancos, Colorado, from Bluff, Utah, by Peter Allen, the mail carrier.

According to Allen, for many months William Ross, formerly of Blum & Ross in Durango, had lived with Hasjkéneinii, a prominent Navajo headman and owner of the Pish-la-ki mine. Ross finally succeeded in getting the trust of Haskéneinii, and the Indian had taken him to the mine. Ross brought the news to Bluff just before Allen left for Mancos, and then returned to the discovery at once. Significantly, Allen concluded by stating that Ross was accompanied by Cass Hite.[11]

First of all, significant is the fact that the Pish-la-ki silver had evidently not been shown to Ross. Nothing ever developed from his story, and nothing further was heard of his supposed find. Secondly, this account by Ross sounds suspiciously similar to that later recounted by Hite, his relatives, and Cy Warman, the newspaper correspondent and writer. Either Hite later took Ross' story and attributed it to himself, or Hashkéneinii had no compunctions about adopting white prospectors as his son or making them a blood brother. It may very well have been that Hashkéneinii was simply following the old adage of "Keep your friends close, and your enemies closer." While he or his son were with any hopeful prospectors, they could make sure that none of them came too close to the actual location of the Navajos' silver deposit.

Still another party of prospectors to the Navajo country in the summer of 1883 was revealed to a Denver newspaper reporter in December of that year. Charles T. Johnson, a prospector and miner, had arrived in Denver to supposedly procure the needed equipment to develop a rich vein of ore that he had recently discovered. According to his remarkable, and ultimately unbelievable story, early the past summer a party of prospectors, of which Johnson was a member, started out to find the immense, what he called "gold," deposit that had been discovered by Myrick and Mitchell. After two weeks of forced march, during which many detours had to be made to avoid gaping canyons with which the plateau was seamed, they finally reached Navajo Mountain.

They began their search cautiously, but not encountering any Indians, they soon divided up into small parties and made a somewhat thorough investigation of the surrounding country. However, for a long time they were without success.

Then one day Johnson became separated from the party to which he was attached. He soon found himself in a forest of fallen and tangled timber through which it was impossible to ride. Johnson then tethered his horse to a large tree and started out on foot. He had not gone far when he suddenly stepped upon some loose brush and found himself falling down a steep incline. Upon reaching the bottom he discovered he was in a sort of cave, which he soon ascertained was actually the underground workings of a mine. Johnson lit a candle, which he fortuitously had brought with him, and almost immediately came upon a vein of pure white quartz. It was evenly seamed with what he knew at once was gold. Johnson returned to the foot of the shaft he had slid down but was unable to climb back up its precipitous side. He began to shout at the top of his voice and soon heard an answering cry from his companions. A rope was soon lowered, and he was pulled up to the surface.

The entire party camped at the spot that night and the next day several more of the prospectors were lowered into the shaft. They all confirmed what Johnson had seen, but after due consideration they realized that at the present time they had no means of capitalizing upon his find. They would have to return to Colorado for the proper equipment.[12]

Like William Ross' story that same summer, nothing more was heard about Johnson's supposed discovery. More than likely it all was but a ruse to hopefully interest potential investors in a further search for gold or silver riches.

However, prospectors did still keep coming to the Navajo Mountain region. In 1927 the party of traveler and explorer Charles L. Bernheimer of New York City discovered a carved inscription over a small cave along the bottom of Chaiyahi Creek, a tributary of Navajo Canyon south of the mountain. It reportedly read: "R.E. Alrod [Allred?] Oct. 1883." Longtime Navajo trader John Wetherill, guide of the party, said that the man was a prospector for silver who was killed by the Indians.[13]

On April 7, 1884, a rumor reached the U.S. Indian Agency at Fort Defiance of a recent conflict up to the northwest between some Navajos and a small party of white men. Sam Boo-ko-di, a Navajo Scout, was sent out at once to investigate. His report on April 19 said that two Americans had been camped at one of the low-lying hills to the southeast of Navajo Mountain and were later killed.

About April 21, Pete, another Navajo Scout, was then sent by Agent Denis M. Riordan to Monument Valley to further investigate. His report, dated May 4, confirmed that on or about March 31, the two Americans had been killed by Navajos near Navajo Mountain. It was subsequently learned that the two victims were Samuel Walcott, an elderly man from Baltimore, Maryland, and his young partner, James McNally. Walcott had been prospecting through the San Juan country for some four years, with his headquarters in the mining town of Ouray, Colorado.

The Navajos implicated in the crime were identified as Diné Ts'osi, "Slender Navajo," and Hashkéneinii Biyé. Each placed blame on the other, but it was eventually brought out that Hashkéneinii Biyé had killed Walcott, accidentally or intentionally, during a scuffle over a gun at the prospectors' camp. McNally, who was away gathering their horses at the time, was then trailed for several miles and also slain in an attempt to cover up the crime.[14]

During the latter part of January in 1884, A. Johnson, William Groen, and Victor E. Neff had left Durango on a prospecting trip to the Navajo country of northern Arizona. According to a sworn statement later made by Neff, they went by way of McElmo Creek to the Mitchell ranch on the San Juan River. There they met Walcott and McNally. In early February the five joined up together and left for Arizona. Eventually, Walcott and McNally started back to Mitchell's about a month before the other three. This latter trio arrived at Mitchell's about the 10th or 12th of April, and there learned that Walcott and McNally had been killed by Navajo Indians on or about March 27.[15]

Subsequent letters between Neff and the Walcott family lawyer in Maryland provided additional details. The five prospectors together had left the Mitchell ranch on February 8. They were evidently in search of the Myrick-Mitchell mine, as evidenced by the presence of their camp just southeast of Navajo Mountain. As many before them, they were presumably unsuccessful, as on March 17, Walcott and McNally left the others to investigate some reported copper prospects in Monument

Valley. Upon the remaining three prospectors' departure from Navajo Mountain, Neff said that they followed Walcott and McNally's backtrail for five days, before they eventually lost it near the mouth of Tsegi Canyon.[16]

This latter statement is confirmed by the presence of an inscription left on the wall of Long House Ruin, a prehistoric Anasazi pueblo structure, located just to the southwest of Marsh Pass and the mouth of the Tsegi. It reads: "V. E. Neff 1884."

On August 15 of 1884, the new Navajo Agent, John H. Bowman, and a contingent of Navajo Scouts and U.S. soldiers, left Fort Defiance for the Monument Valley-Navajo Mountain region. Their primary objectives were to try and arrest Hashkéneinii Biyé and to recover the bodies of the two slain prospectors. Hashkéneinii Biyé, however, evaded capture and fled to the protection of a band of renegade Utes to the north. But an old Navajo did lead the group to the shallow burial of Walcott's body. This was reported by Bowman to have been about eight miles from El Capitan and some five miles from the range of hills known as the Haystacks – present-day Agathla Peak and Comb Ridge, respectively. Walcott's grave, then, would have been somewhere in the Kayenta area. McNally was reportedly buried somewhere on the long, high mesa to the south – today's Black Mesa near Chilchinbito, Arizona. But the search party was not able to find any trace of his remains.[17]

Hashkéneinii Biyé, despite several different attempts, was never brought to justice. His father, however, Old Hashkéneinii, was arrested and placed in jail at Fort Wingate, New Mexico, for some seven months. Though innocent of any connection with the unfortunate affair, he was held as a sort of hostage in the U.S. military's desire to apprehend his son. Hashkéneinii Biyé was never made to suffer any consequences for his misdeed, though he did acquire a new name from the affair – At'íní, meaning "The One Who Did It." Even today there are several families in the Navajo Mountain region, descendants of Haskéneinii Biyé, with the last name of Atene, a slightly different spelling of the original.[18]

Modern-day residents of the Navajo Mountain community, such as the Atenes, have little to say about the Pish-la-ki mine. However, a story related by the late Robert Graymountain, and attributed to his father, put the location of the silver deposit near one of two low hills, southeast of Navajo Mountain and north of Jackrabbit Canyon.[19] This sounds remarkably like the location of the last camp of slain prospectors Samuel Walcott and James McNally in 1884.

In this year, 1884, J.P. Williams once again had his hand in the search for the Pish-la-ki mine. In a statement given many years after the fact, one of his sons, William F. Williams, said that he had gone to Navajo Mountain in 1884 in company with his father. Hashkéneinii also went with them, as he insisted that he could show them where the silver prospect was that had been worked by Myrick and Mitchell. However, according to Williams, as it turned out Hashkéneinii did not seem to know much anything about it at all. The Williamses believed that Hashkéneinii, who they contended had never actually seen the place himself, thought he could take them there because he had talked to the Indians who killed Myrick and Mitchell in Monument Valley.

The identity of this Hashkéneinii is not positively known. In actuality, it sounds much more like Hashkéneinii Biyé. who in fact did not know the exact location of the mine site. But if it was the father, the elder Hashkéneinii could very well have simply been leading the Williamses on another of his wild-goose chases.

It was in November of 1884 that the elder Williams, his son, and Hashkéneinii started from El Capitan for Navajo Mountain. They crossed the upper end of Piute Canyon and stayed a couple of days or so with the Paiute Indians that had farms there. Then they went to Nasja Canyon, on the north side of Navajo Mountain. Here, Williams and his father prospected around, while Hashkéneinii tried to obtain more information about the place where Myrick and Mitchell had been. They then climbed up on top of the mountain and after searching there awhile went back down over a sort of intermediate bench to what they called Willow Spring. From there they descended into some of the side canyons of West Canyon, now called Navajo Canyon. Finally, though, in December, the search was given up.

The next year, in 1885, J.P. Williams still believed that silver could be found around Navajo Mountain. This time both of his sons, Bill and Ben, accompanied him, and they set up a small camp near Willow Spring, probably today's Rainbow Lodge Spring. While there they also visited the Inscription House Ruin. According to Bill they left their names and the date nearby, and in fact there is still an inscription there which reads: "W. Williams 1885." They stayed for a while at Willow Spring, but eventually got discouraged and left for home.[20]

In a story by Gladwell Richardson, who interviewed Bill Williams many years later, while they were at Willow Springs, the Williamses encouraged local Indians to bring in samples of rock that they thought might be mineralized. These were kept in a burlap sack and largely forgotten about. But upon returning to Blue Canyon, one specimen was found to be rich in gold. However, by then it was impossible to identify where or from whom that particular piece of ore had come.[21]

One of the many names and dates at Inscription House Ruin reads: "John Hadley Nov. 17 1885." Another inscription, "W.R. Robins Jul 2 1887," is found at the ever-popular watering stop of Tse Ya Toe Spring. Both are undoubtedly indications of prospectors searching for the Lost Myrick and Mitchell Silver Mine. White men would have had no other reason to be in the Navajo Mountain region during those times.

In the fall of 1887, Joe Smith, C.C. Duff, Dave Aleerly, and E.J. Johnson, all residents of southwestern Colorado, organized themselves to go down and look for the Pish-la-ki silver mine in the Navajo country. Writing years later, Johnson said that they started from the Noland Trading Post, on the San Juan River in the far southeast corner of Utah, with a pack outfit of burros. Their trip took them down the north side of the San Juan about forty or fifty miles to a crossing, undoubtedly the Mules Ear Crossing near the old Barton trading post. Late in the afternoon of the third day south of the river, they came within sight of the peak which Johnson called the Big Capitan, today's Agathla Peak. It was recognized as the principal monument in Monument Valley and was the first landmark on the way to the mine.

The next night the quartet of prospectors reached the base of the Big Capitan and the following morning started toward the next landmark, Mitchell Butte, a few miles away. Upon arrival there they supposedly found evidence of the last camping place of Myrick and Mitchell. Their direction from that point was southwest several miles to the mouth of a deep canyon, probably Tseyi-hatsosi. This canyon was entered by a well-worn Indian trail which was supposed to lead down to water about one mile below and then on to the mine.

About a mile away was a single small butte, and the prospectors now noticed two horsemen near it. Upon looking around in all directions there were now seen other mounted natives, reportedly standing still like sentinels. Soon, two of the Indians eventually came forward to meet them. One spoke quite good English and asked Johnson and the others where they were going, what they wanted, and what they were searching for? They answered that they were just looking around exploring. Then the Indian stated that this was no place for white men and that they must go back the way they had come. He concluded by saying that they could go and look around anywhere else, but not off to the south, upcanyon. The prospectors took him at his word and reportedly explored farther to the west and among the cliff dwellers' ruins before they finally returned to Colorado.[22]

This latter statement is confirmed by two inscriptions, one at Long House Ruin near the mouth of Tsegi Canyon, and the other at the often-visited Inscription House Ruin. In both locations there is scratched the name "C. C. Duff," one of Johnson's three companions.

The decade of the 1880s came to a close with still the occasional prospector to the Navajo country. No longer to be seen, but reported in 1924, was the name "G.R. Choistian" and date of "Oct. 24, 1888" at Inscription House Ruin.[23] There is also still present a "Geo. E. Christensen Sep 10 1889" inscription at Tse Ya Toe Spring.

But the lure of the Lost Myrick and Mitchell Silver Mine continued to live on. As Heber Christensen said in 1934, "I do not think there is any question as to the famous Pish-la-ki mine. I have heard Mr. Frank Hyde, of Bluff, Utah, tell the story of his father, William Hyde, placing 1,500 silver dollars on a blanket and offering it to a Navajo to show him where the mine was. But the Indian only laughed and said that he could dig [up] that much in just one hour."[24]

J.P. Williams family
Jonathan Williams, seated center, William F. Williams, standing at left
Courtesy of Billie Williams Yost

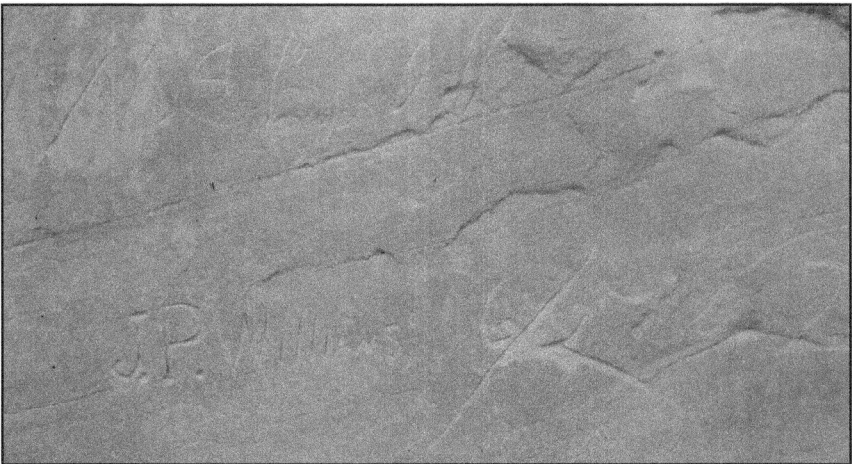

J.P. Williams 6/2 82
Aztec Creek, Forbidding Canyon

Evergreens and downfall, Top of Navajo Mountain

Tseyi-hatsosi Canyon

Ten:

The Next Decade

If, as English essayist Alexander Pope stated, "Hope springs eternal in the human breast," then so it must also reside in the heart of many an old-time prospector. And the search for the legendary Pish-ka-ki silver mine of the Navajos was no exception. Although ten years had passed since the deaths of Myrick and Mitchell and no further trace of the mine had yet been found, prospectors unabatedly continued in their quest for its riches.

One of the most persistent of these searchers was Joseph A. Duckett. Born in 1848 at the foot of the Great Smoky Mountains in western North Carolina, he and his family moved to the Wet Mountain Valley of south-central Colorado in the early 1870s.[1] As indicated in earlier chapters, Duckett was evidently at the Mitchell store at the mouth of McElmo Creek when Charles Myrick passed by late in 1879 and was also still there a short time later when he, luckily as it turned out, missed out on an opportunity to accompany Myrick on his last, fateful trip. He was, however, a member of three later prospecting expeditions that did indeed search for the elusive silver mine from 1881 until 1883. After the failure of the Copper Canyon mines in 1883, that fall, following the forceable expulsion of the native Utes, the entire Duckett family moved to the newly opened Grand Valley of western Colorado.[2]

In early December of 1890, Joe Duckett, his two brothers, John and Thaddeus, and six other fellow ranchers from the Grand Valley region departed on a nearly three-month search for the Myrick and Mitchell silver mine. Whose idea it was for the expedition is not known, but Joe was the nominal leader from the start based on his previous experience in various searches for the long-sought silver deposit. The group traveled to the Navajo country by way of Moab, Monticello, and Bluff, all small Mormon towns in southeastern Utah.

Unlike most earlier searches for the mine, which approached the Navajo Mountain region from Monument Valley, Duckett believed that the site could be better accessed by descending the San Juan River and then following up one of its southern tributary canyons to the area of the mountain. But after an aborted attempt by way of Foote Canyon (present-day Nokai) and East Canyon Mesa (today's Piute Mesa), the nine-man group finally trekked overland westward from Copper Canyon, across Nokai Mesa and Canyon, to Piute Mesa via the native Moonlight Water Trail. There they spent some thirteen days in a futile search in various directions and down into different side canyons for the Navajo silver mine.

Finally, on January 30 of 1891, the prospectors must have finally gotten close to their goal. Joe Duckett wanted to go down into East, or Piute Canyon, in a last-ditch search effort. Up until this time the local Paiute and Navajo had proved inoffensive and even friendly, but on this occasion things took a different turn. The women, children, and sheep were sent down the canyon, while the braves took up positions in the rocks that lined both of its sides. When the prospectors entered a smaller tributary gorge, perhaps today's Jackrabbit Canyon, on the west side of the main canyon, two of the Indians came down and joined them on their march. After a short while the pair of natives then went on ahead.

The group of white men stopped and finally decided to not attempt to proceed any farther. They returned to their camp, and the entire party started back for Colorado the next day. No valuable mineral had been found, and certainly not the Pish-la-ki mine. However, perhaps the legendary silver deposit was, in fact, not that far away. The last day's defensive behavior of the local Navajos may very well have indicated as much.[3]

But Joe Duckett was nothing if not persistent. Either alone, or sometimes with his brother, John B. Duckett, he continued to search for the Myrick-Mitchell mine off and on until well into the 1900s. One story handed down through the Duckett family, though a date is not given, has Joe down on the Navajo reservation in a little side canyon draining north to the San Juan River near Navajo Mountain, still in search of the elusive silver. Before he realized they were there, a band of Navajos suddenly surrounded him and displayed a very threatening attitude. Duckett feared for his life, but thought quickly and began to act like a crazy man. He walked in circles, waved his arms, and jerked his head up and down and side to side. There was supposedly an Indian superstition that it was bad luck indeed to harm a person who had been "touched in the head by the Great Spirit." Desperately counting on this belief, Duckett continued his charade, now babbling incoherently. Finally, the Navajos let him go on his way, but not without first sternly warning him to never come back to the Navajo country.[4]

However, Duckett did, in fact, continue to return. Sometime in the 1890s or early in the 1900s, Joe and his brother, John, made yet another attempt at locating the lost silver of Myrick and Mitchell. For years Joe, sometimes with John, on a purely practical basis would go down into the Navajo reservation to trap animals for their hides and pelts. But another, underlying, purpose was to keep their eyes and ears open for any indication of the long-sought silver mine.

According to one story, the Duckett brothers had spent nearly all of one season trapping and looking for the mine, but it was now almost springtime, and they would soon have to give up the search and return to their farming and ranching duties. They had brought in their traps, and on this particular day they had gone up a more isolated, very steep canyon. About midday a heavy rain and subsequent hailstorm forced them to take shelter in a shallow cave for an hour or two. When the storm finally blew over, the two brothers decided to return to their camp, as there was not enough time left to go any farther and still get back before darkness fell.

Several years later Joe happened upon one of his Navajo friends in town, and during the ensuing conversation the Indian asked why he and his brother had stopped coming down to the reservation. Joe replied that he was getting too old and would never go again. He also admitted that they had been looking for the Pish-la-ki silver mine all along and used the trapping as a decoy. After a thoughtful pause, the Indian then answered that the Navajos had known all along that the two brothers had been searching for the mine, and that someone had always been watching and keeping an eye on them. He then reminded Joe of the time he and his brother were going up a narrow canyon and a storm forced them to take cover in a cave, and after it stopped they turned around and went back to their camp. The Navajo then solemnly stated that on that day, if the rain had not come, the two brothers would have gotten close enough to the storied mine that they both would had to have been killed.[5]

Winslow Wetherill was the youngest of the five Wetherill brothers, and like most of his siblings was involved in the trading post business for much of his life. From 1914 until 1918, he operated a small store at what the Navajos called Covered Water west of Chinle, Arizona, at the foot of Black Mesa. Later in life, his wife, Hilda Faunce, wrote a book about her life at various trading posts on the Navajo reservation based on letters that she had written at the time. One of these told a story of what Ms. Faunce called "Guarded Gold," though it certainly has overtones of the Myrick-Mitchell silver.

While at Covered Water, in 1917, a Navajo from far to the north, the Navajo Mountain area, visited the store. One of the local natives said that this man, whom he called Tsay-Nez, or "Tall Rock," was the longtime "enforcer" for the guarding of the Navajo gold [sic]. Upon inquiry, the following tale was related.

Maybe twenty-five years earlier, which would have placed it in the early 1890s, two white men came to the northern Navajo country. They were surreptitiously followed, and at one place they dug into a hillside and then filled several canvas sacks with certain rocks. When Hashkéneinii was informed of this, he said that the two men were looking for the Navajos' gold. The next night, when they had reached Monument Valley, Hashkéneinii went to them and directed them to water. Later, while the two slept in their camp, Hashkéneinii took an axe and killed both of the white prospectors. Their horses and mules were driven away, their equipment scattered about, and the canvas bags emptied of their rock samples.

A day later Hashkéneinii was informed that seven more whites were approaching. He and some his braves rode out to meet them and were told they were looking for two of their companions who had traveled on ahead of their party. Hashkéneinii said that these other two had been killed, but that two of the present group would be permitted to come and bury them. When this was done, the chosen two searchers took with them the canvas sacks, which still contained some dust and broken rock fragments. They then returned to the others, and the entire party went back north and crossed the San Juan River. All the way they were shadowed by Hashkéneinii and his braves.

Afterward, Hashkéneinii declared that white men should never be allowed to take samples from the Navajos' mine and that the place should always be guarded. Any whites who got too close to the place would be killed. This task was entrusted to Tsay-Nez.[6]

When this story is compared to earlier accounts of the Pish-la-ki mine, it is obvious that it is actually a combination of several different events in the history of the Navajo silver lode. The two white prospectors could very well have been Myrick and Mitchell, and their collecting samples of ore and being directed to water by Hashkéneinii certainly agrees with previous stories. But the subsequent killing of the two men with an axe by Hashkéneinii is no doubt a recollection of the slaying of Walcott and McNally by Hashkéneinii Biyé. The allowing of two members of the following search party to come in and bury the two bodies is reminiscent of Cass Hite and one companion being allowed by Hashkéneinii to recover the bodies of Myrick and Mitchell. Faunce's story, however, does ultimately substantiate the decision by Hashkéneinii to never allow any white prospectors to get near their Pish-la-ki mine.

In the summer of 1892, a brief article appeared in the Flagstaff, Arizona, newspaper that told of another search for the lost silver mine. A man named James W. Black had just returned earlier in the week from a trip to the Navajo country to the northeast toward Navajo Mountain. But after a two-week search through rocky canyons and enduring the excessive heat at that season, he was forced to abandon his search and return to a "shady place and ice water."[7]

Later in the fall of that same year, placer gold deposits were discovered along the San Juan River to the northeast of Navajo Mountain. The ensuing "San Juan excitement" lasted from December, 1892 until February, 1893. The resulting "rush," which brought in hundreds, some say thousands, of hopeful miners, was, of course, for the fine gold and larger nuggets in the sands of the river. However, when the short-lived excitement soon died down, some of the disappointed prospectors turned their attention to the surrounding country, including Navajo

Mountain. Some searched for the possible source of the placer gold, while others remembered the story of the Myrick and Mitchell silver. Either way, subsequent stories of the Navajos' Pish-la-ki mine would now sometimes involve gold as well as silver.

An article in one of the Salt Lake City newspapers in 1935 recounted a story about a gold [sic] lode on Navajo Mountain. Geshi Canyon is one of the longer eastern tributaries in the upper part of Navajo Canyon and was named for a Navajo by that name who lived near its mouth. In this account Geshi was one of the discoverers of the gold lode. At some point in time two educated Indians took samples of this mineral to a nearby town. They proved to be exceptionally high-grade ore, and three white men subsequently started back with the two Indians. But before they ever reached the mine, all were shot to death, reportedly by Geshi.[8]

On August 22, 1892, J.J. Mackey, John Lee, Frank Serrier, Lon Morton, Charles Frederick, and P.A. Craig located a mining prospect in the Abajo Mountains west of Monticello, Utah, in the southeastern part of the then territory. The claim was filed at the courthouse in Monticello on September 14.[9] What is significant about this is that five of the six men had also left their names, and in two cases the date, far to the southwest at Tse Ya Toe Spring. Craig's inscription was dated "Aug. 4, 1892," eighteen days before the strike in the Abajos. Evidently the group had come to Utah by way of the Navajo Mountain region and were probably looking for the Pish-la-ki mine along the way.

Sometime in the 1940s an old prospector named Albert M. Rogers then lived near Monticello and told the following story to neighbor Clarence A. Frost. Rogers had come into the San Juan country during the gold excitement of 1892-93 and like so many others had stayed around after the rush had abated. He had heard of the reported rich silver deposit out on the Navajo reservation, and also that Hashkéneinii, the headman of the area, was the guardian of the mine. Consequently, Rogers traveled to the Navajo's camp and asked if he could stay there with them. He reportedly lived there for four years and supposedly was eventually granted the privilege to see the mine.

Rogers was put on a horse and blindfolded and then led an estimated four miles. Upon arrival he was taken from the horse, and the bandana removed from his eyes. The first thing he saw was an old wooden and leather bellows, which had been used to blow fire to melt silver from the rocks. He was told that the Navajo no longer used the mine, as they now utilized silver coins for the making of their jewelry. The site was presently used as a bedding ground for sheep and goats, to cover up all traces of the former silver ore.

Then Rogers was shown seven skeletons lying in a row. From the remnants of their footwear he could tell they were white men. The Navajos ultimately told him in no uncertain terms that if he ever attempted to come back to that place, his body would be laid beside those bones already there. Later Rogers described the site as being in a very rough place, not down in a canyon, but on more of a hillside or "rimrock side-hill."[10]

Rogers' story, of course, is much like the accounts given earlier about similar-sounding experiences with Hashkéneinii – those of Cass Hite and William Ross. However, at least the actual presence of Rogers in the area is shown by an inscription he left at Tse Ya Toe Spring that reads: "A.M. Rogers Feb.16, 1893 Rico, Colo." This would have been near the end of the San Juan gold rush.

In a statement given many years later, prospector James W. Black said that in January of 1894, he and two other men, Al Brown and George McDowell, quit their placer gold mining on the San Juan and moved toward Navajo Mountain. They worked up the mountain onto the top from the eastern-most flank, where there was less snow. They then camped on the lee side of what would later be called Lookout Ridge and built a large fire. This blaze was seen by a lone prospector who was spending the winter on the mountain but was unable to prospect at the time because of the depth of snow in the surrounding timber. His name was Patterson, no first name given, and was judged to be about sixty-five years old. Black and his companions' time was limited by their food supply, so they eventually came away from the mountain by way of the so-called East Trail, an old Indian route.[11]

Neither Black and his two fellow prospectors, or Patterson, would have had any real reason for being up on Navajo Mountain unless they were, in fact, looking for the Myrick and Mitchell silver mine. An inscription reading "J. Arnold 1894," is also found at Inscription House Ruin. This is possibly still another seeker after the Pish-la-ki mine.

In 1913, geologist Herbert E. Gregory found an old wooden stake on top of Navajo Mountain in a clearing among the surrounding spruce trees. It read: "Ford 1896 Apr. 22."[12] Very likely this was yet another hopeful prospector.

Also in April of 1896, an incident took place which concerned the Myrick and Mitchell mine. At that time the Palmer family of Illinois was being guided by Richard Wetherill, eldest of the five brothers, from Flagstaff to the Wetherill's Alamo Ranch near Mancos, Colorado. Part of their journey lay along what they called the Elk Mountain Fault, actually present-day Comb Ridge between Kayenta, Arizona, and the San Juan River. One day they came to a cave along the upturned ridge and decided to camp there for the night.

Soon members of the party began to find pieces of very rich silver ore said to be soft enough that they could cut it with a knife. They gathered several specimens and took them along on their journey. Perhaps significantly, the following day they came to the camp of Hashkéneinii. When they eventually arrived at the San Juan River, they crossed over and soon entered the town of Bluff. There they were told that the cave where they found the mineral was where the Indians had killed Myrick and Mitchell.[13]

Later, daughter Marietta Palmer married Richard Wetherill, and almost sixty years afterward, in 1953, told of the above incident during an interview. This seems to be the first occasion that the killing of the two prospectors was placed at a location somewhere other than in Monument Valley. To be geographically accurate, while Comb Ridge is considered to be the eastern boundary of Monument Valley, it is several miles from the Mitchell and Merrick Buttes where the two prospectors were actually slain. It is also somewhat strange that if, in fact, the Bluff townspeople did know of the cave, why they themselves had not long before gathered up all of the available rich silver ore supposedly scattered about there. Likely, either the Bluff folk, or Marietta herself, were simply concocting an entertaining story.

Inspired by a party that was getting together for the purpose of making still another search for the Pish-la-ki mine, a lengthy article appeared in one of the Salt Lake City newspapers in the spring of 1897 that purportedly gave the origins of the legend. It is a good example of what by then, nearly two decades after the event, had become a bewildering mixture of fact, fantasy, and a combination of what were actually several separate episodes.

First of all, the article is titled "The Lost Merrick Gold Mine," silver never being mentioned. Secondly, it stated that the mine was found in Copper Canyon. The article, unsigned, then went on to say that Merrick [sic], after he had made camp in the canyon, went out to search for water. He became lost and was compelled to spend the night in a cave. Scattered around was a lot of mineral ore, literally held together by wires of free gold. Merrick took samples with him and finally made his way to the mining camps of southwest Colorado.

There he took a man by the name of Mitchell into his confidence, and they made plans to return for more of the valuable ore. Just before they started, Mitchell informed a friend of his in the strictest confidence that Merrick had told him that the mine was in what was known as West Canyon, one of the canyons leading into Copper Canyon.

While in the Colorado mining camps, Merrick's somewhat mysterious actions aroused the suspicions of several of the townspeople, and when it was learned that he had started out on his trip, it was only two days later that a party of fifteen prospectors took the trail after him and Mitchell. The names given were John Sessions and Bill Matthews of Parrott City, Noah Barnes of McElmo Canyon, a Mr. Rives of Ouray, Charles Smith, Tom Moore, Martin Rush of Mancos, Bill Clemens, J.H. McCracken of Cortez, Nat Kilbourne of Mancos, Jim Kevelin, Doc Winters of Durango, H.M. Smith of Mancos, Charles Clamhurst, and J.J. Weed of Dolores, Colorado.

This large party, however, soon lost the trail and spent several days casting about until they struck it once again. Finally, they arrived in Monument Valley and came across the body of Mitchell, apparently the day after he was killed. The search was continued, and Merrick's body was eventually found in Moonlight Canyon, described as one of the darkest and most dismal gorges in the region. The party then hunted for the supposed gold mine for several weeks before they ran out of food and were forced to return to Colorado.[14]

While a group of prospectors from Rico and the surrounding region did in fact start on the trail of Myrick and Mitchell, it was over two weeks later, not two days. And while they did indeed find the body of Hernan Mitchell in Monument Valley, Charles Myrick's was not found miles to the west in Moonlight – today's Oljeto Canyon – but only two or three miles to the north at today's Merrick Butte. The initial search party, comprised of Mitchell's father and a few other men from the McElmo area, did soon run out of supplies and were forced to curtail their rescue efforts. However, the larger party described in this 1897 article was more than likely the expedition launched later and which spanned the winter of 1880-81. Moonlight, or Oljeto, Canyon is actually fairly wide and open along most of its length, certainly not dark and dismal as described. Finally, there is the statement that the "lost Merrick mine" was found in West Canyon, a branch of Copper Canyon. This undoubtedly came from the fact that Cass Hite's Merrick and Mitchell *copper* mine was located in what is shown as the West Fork of Copper Canyon on modern maps of the area.

Therefore, by the end of the 1800s, fact and fancy were already being confused in the Pish-la-ki and Myrick-Mitchell mine legend.

Joseph A. Duckett, Late 1800's
Courtesy of Thaddeus Duckett family

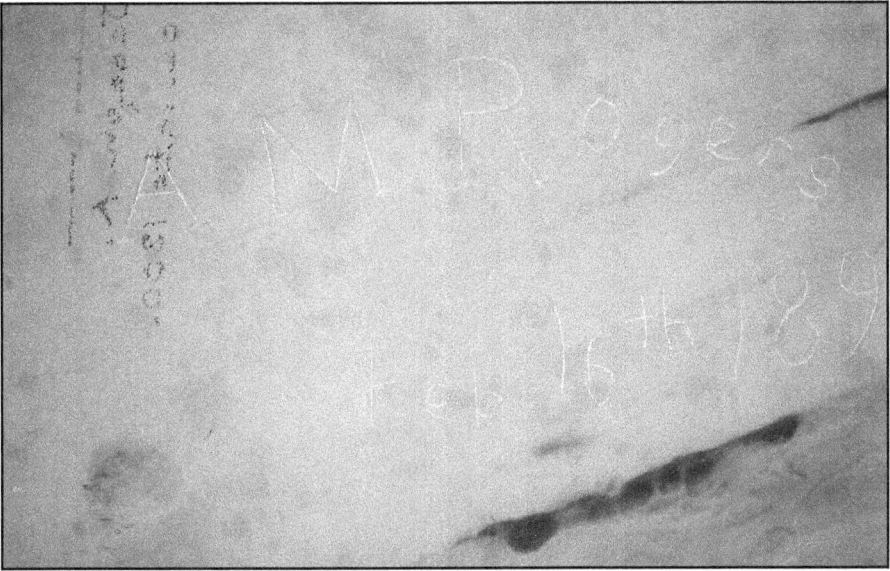

A.M. Rogers, Feb 16th 1893
Tse Ya Toe Spring

Upper Copper Canyon

Eleven:
The 20th Century

A new century seemed to bring about a lessening in the search for the Pish-la-ki silver mine, though it did not stop entirely. One man who continued explorations after his first exposure to the Navajo mine story in 1879 was Louisa Wetherill's father, John J. "Jack" Wade.

Testifying in 1929, John Wetherill stated that he and his father-in-law had made a search for the lost Myrick and Mitchell mine in the fall of 1900. Their particular area of interest was in Adahchijiyahi Canyon, one of the series of canyons that cut into the plateau region that separates Monument Valley and Navajo Mountain. Nothing, however, was found.[1] Interestingly, this canyon is the principal western tributary of Tseyi-hatsosi Canyon, where prospector E.J. Johnson and his three companions were forbidden from visiting back in 1887.

In 1901, Wade and Wetherill tried again. Wade described a large body of intrusive rock that he had found in the Oljeto area back in 1892, and he believed that it might contain valuable ore. But once again their trip was destined for failure. They could not even find the intrusion that Wade remembered. However, the following year their persistent efforts were finally successful. Along with John's younger brother, Clayton Wetherill, as well as John Clark and Frank Lime, they found the intrusive body that Wade had recalled. They took samples of the rock back to an assayer, but were informed that it contained no valuable minerals.[2]

The Adahchijiyahi – Tseyi-hotsosi canyon system has long been one of the supposed locations of the Pish-la-ki mine. Sometime in the late 1800s or early 1900s (no specific date is given), brothers Sam and Charley Day had their turn in seeking that area's purported mineral wealth. The two were sons of longtime Navajo trader Samuel Day of Chinle, Arizona, who had been in the Chinle Valley area since the 1870s. Through overheard comments and conversational talk made at their father's trading post by visiting Navajo patrons, the two brothers gradually learned of what Sam Day II said were "rich gold deposits" in Tseyi-hatsosi Canyon.

The Day brothers proceeded to make the long pack trip westward across the desolate Chinle Valley, past the towering ramparts of Black Mesa, and finally to the wide drainage of Oljeto, or Moonlight Water, Creek. The broad mouth of Tseyi-hatsosi Canyon lay just a few miles to the south. They traveled deep into that canyon until they reached the section where it "started to break." This may have been where Adahchijiyahi Canyon branches off to the west. Here they began to make camp near a small, rocky knoll.

The brothers soon noticed something whitish-colored at the foot of this hill. Upon examination they found that it was the skeleton of a burro and the bleached bones of a man. Scattered around were the remains of a pack. It was obviously a prospector who had failed to solve the riddle of Navajo gold, and fearful of the same fate, the Days quickly resaddled their horses, packed up their camp, and left as fast as they could.[3]

Perhaps this story ties in with one published in 1911. Years earlier, so the story went, an Easterner from Yale was determined to find the silver of the *Diné*. He went to the Navajo country, married a native woman, learned their language, reared a family, and after sixteen years of patient waiting was finally told of its location. Certain of the inevitable discovery he went back to the East, secured a financial backer, and then returned to the Navajo country. He hired the services of a number of local cowboys and set out for the mine. However, they were heard of no more. Years afterward the remains of the entire party were found. Their skeletons had been laid out in a row, and their skulls pillowed on boulders.[4] There are echoes of this account in the story told by prospector Albert M. Rogers in the preceding chapter.

In later years an account concerning the Pish-la-ki mine was told by Bluff resident Frank Hyde. Around 1906, he said, he and a mining man from Denver believed there was a possibility that even if all of the easily obtained silver had been removed from the Navajo mine, enough low-grade ore might still remain to make it profitable to be worked. Subsequently, they convinced Hashkéneinii Biyé, though he told them emphatically that there was "nothing there," to take the engineer out and show him the mine for the sum of twenty-five dollars. Indeed, the Denver professional did find ore pockets scattered throughout an exposure of conglomerate rock. However, they had all been "cleaned out." All that remained was a small amount of melted slag lying on the ground and some medium-grade ore that barely filled a handkerchief.[5]

Hashkéneinii Biyé always steadfastly maintained that he himself never knew the exact location of the Pish-la-ki mine. Therefore, the above story, if true, is but yet another example of the Navajo father and son simply taking advantage of white hopefuls' greed and gullibility and fleecing them for whatever they could in the way of monetary payment.

John Wetherill and Louisa Wade were married in 1896, and ten years later, in 1906, they moved far to the northwest to the Oljeto area, where they were given permission to establish a trading post by the local "headman," Hashkéneinii. Some maintain that one of their objectives was to get closer to the location of the rumored Pish-la-ki silver mine of the Navajos.[6] Indeed, a letter from William T. Shelton, U.S. Indian agent of the recently established San Juan Agency at Shiprock, New Mexico, to John Wetherill in the fall of 1906, inquired about a man at their new Oljeto home who was reported to be prospecting for the Myrick-Mitchell mine.[7] Perhaps this was the Denver mining man spoken of by Frank Hyde.

Hashkéneinii died in 1909. Shortly before his death he sent word to Louisa Wetherill to come to his hogan, as he had something of great importance to tell her. However, when she arrived, he was feeling somewhat better, so he postponed whatever pronouncement he had intended to make. Just a few days later, though, the Navajo headman did pass away. Whatever of importance that he had wished to convey to Louisa was now lost, but some believe that Hashkéneinii intended to divulge the location of the Pish-la-ki mine to his adopted white daughter.[8]

It was perhaps around this time that the Navajo silver lode was thought to have been hidden away from all inquisitive eyes. According to Hashkéneinii Biyé's 1939 interview, only his father and six other tribal elders knew the location of the mine, and they were all now dead. Arthur H. Spencer said that when he owned and operated a trading post in the early 1900s at Mexican Hat, Utah, on the San Juan River, he became friends with Hashkéneinii Biyé. He reportedly told Spencer that while he himself had never been to the mine, supposedly a half-breed Paiute and a Navajo now lived there and had made a sheep corral over the site.[9]

Spencer then added the important fact that he also had become acquainted with the Indians that had killed Myrick and Mitchell. The two he named were Mike's Boy and Joe Bush. One day he was out on the Navajo reservation buying sheep, supposedly in the general region of the Pish-la-ki mine. Upon his return to his trading post that evening he inquired of the two Paiutes if they actually knew where the old silver mine was located. They laughed and said that he had walked over it that very day while out buying sheep. Of course, Spencer had been to several different sheep camps that day, and therefore had no really good idea where the mine might have been.[10]

According to Hilda Faunce, the wife of Winslow Wetherill, in August of 1917 a lone white man rode up to their store at Covered Water, on the western edge of the Chinle Valley. Though in her published book Ms. Faunce used pseudonyms, not only for her husband but for this solitary visitor as well, it is quite obvious to whom she referred. The stranger said that his name was Merrill (actually Myrick), and he wanted to buy some feed for his horses and camp nearby for the night.

Later that evening the man related that he was from Texas and that years ago his older brother had been in this country and discovered some very rich "gold" ore. The Indians had killed him and his partner, but the story had eventually gotten out and ever since had been handed down through his family. Now, he was there to find that gold. Myrick continued on with his story and said that one of the two men whom the Indians had later guided in to bury his brother and companion had come back to Texas years afterward and told the whole story. That gentleman had also drawn a map of where the graves had been, and which were said to be but a one day's ride from the gold.

Several Navajos had lounged around the store all the while this tale was being told. Immediately afterward they all left together and hurried away. The following morning "Merrill," aka Myrick, departed early, headed for Monument Valley. Three days later a Navajo came into the store with a sheet of paper in his hand. He told the Wetherills that the stranger had ridden "straight," as if he knew the trail he wanted to follow. Myrick had made marks on this paper, which proved to be the map that he had spoken about. He had made no wrong turns and evidently knew the way from the graves to the gold.

The prospector never returned to the store and nothing further was ever heard of him. With the possession of his map by the Navajos, the Wetherills were convinced that he had been killed because of his knowledge.[11]

This story by Ms. Faunce, as unlikely as it may seem, does, however, contain some significant points. This Myrick's having an older brother sounds somewhat similar to the "uncle" that the original Myrick was supposed to have had in some of the early 1880s newspaper articles about the Pish-la-ki silver mine. And Cass Hite, one of the two men allowed in by Hashkéneinii to bury the bodies of the two slain prospectors, did in fact live for a time in the Panhandle region of Texas.

In 1922 or 1923, the Frost family lived in the little town of Bluff, Utah, on the San Juan River. While there an elderly man had approached the father, Clarence A. Frost, and convinced him to go along on a trapping expedition for animal pelts and furs down into the Navajo country. They traveled several miles each day, and every evening set out their traps before continuing on the next morning. However, Frost soon began to notice that the Old Man, as he called him, seemed to be in an unusual hurry, even when they happened upon good trapping grounds. He also noticed that the old gentleman obviously knew the country and had evidently been there before.

One day, as they traveled closer to Navajo Mountain, they came to a sort of divide. Up until this time the local Navajos had been very friendly, but now all of that changed. That night, on the north side of this divide, fifteen heavily armed Navajo men came to their camp and acted sullen and threatening. They ignored Frost, but each one pointedly came up and asked the elderly man what he was doing there. The band of *Diné* did not actually wait for any sort of answer, and they then quickly rode away. The Old Man had now become very frightened, and immediately the next morning insisted that they return to Bluff at once. On the way he finally told Frost his story.

Years before he had been in that region hunting for the Myrick-Mitchell silver mine. One day he had entered a new canyon, isolated, in very rough country. It met the description he had heard of the mine's location, but then Indians had suddenly surrounded him. They eventually let him go, but first made him promise never to come back there again or face being killed. Now, however, he was much older and looked very different. He also thought that the natives who had originally driven him out were now either dead or moved elsewhere. However, someone along the way had evidently recognized him.[12]

This story sounds very much like what happened to Joe Duckett and his party at the end of their 1890-91 winter expedition to look for the Navajo silver mine. The Frosts were neighbors of Joe Duckett in the 1920s and early 1930s, and at that time Duckett would, indeed, have been an "old man." The "divide" that was mentioned could very well have been the narrow neck of land that separates Piute and Navajo Canyons, south of Navajo Mountain.

In the early 1920s, Ray Dunn owned and operated the trading post at Chilchinbito, Arizona, at the foot of Black Mesa and not far south of Kayenta. In later years one of his daughters, Madelene Dunn Cameron, during an interview related the following story. In 1922 or 1923 an old prospector had stopped at their store for supplies. He said that he was headed northwest for Navajo Mountain to find gold [sic] that was "in a canyon with only one cottonwood tree." The Dunns never saw or heard of him again.[13]

In 1924 the Richardson family of Flagstaff, Arizona, established what they called Rainbow Lodge at the southern foot of Navajo Mountain, near what the early prospectors had named Willow Spring. Sometime in the next year or so, not far to the south near what is today known as Haystack Rock, two mounds of piled stones were noticed. A son, Gladwell "Toney" Richardson, believed them to mark a gravesite. He dug into one and, indeed, it did turn out to be a burial.

Writing later, Richardson said that beneath the rocks, short pieces of axe-cut cedar covered the actual dug-out hole. They rested on a six-inch bed of hardpan dirt left all around the sides of the pit. The skeleton in the grave had a bullet hole through the skull. Very little cloth or leather was left, but metal buttons and a belt buckle remained. A cartridge belt and gun had been placed at the head of the grave, the bullet casings covered with verdigris and the revolver with rust. Just under them had been placed two twenty-dollar gold pieces dated in the 1870s.

Richardson knew that the placement of the coins and the gun was an old Navajo custom, though it would have been most unusual for any *Diné* to have handled, much less buried, a dead body. But he did surmise that the remains were that of still another unlucky prospector.[14]

In the late 1920s, John Wetherill once again set out in search of the Myrick and Mitchell mine. Hashkéneinii Biyé had told him that he could take him to the place where the two prospectors had worked. He led Wetherill to *Naakii Kíkonillkáadi*, shown as The Ramp on modern maps. This slanting talus slope was the location of an old Navajo trail that led from the Kayenta area to the top of Hoskinnini Mesa. However, the excavated hole, which was indeed there, revealed nothing of value.[15]

About 1932, Joe Duckett played one last hand in the gamble for the Myrick-Mitchell silver mine. He was now getting up in years, feeling rather poorly, and even believed that he was close to dying. He asked Ray Lynn Hyde, an in-law, to come see him and proceeded to relate to him a verbal description of what he believed was the approximate location of the mine. This knowledge came from the occasion when he and his brother had turned back to camp after being halted by a torrential storm and were later informed by a Navajo friend that they were indeed getting close to the area of the silver mine.

Joe Duckett did, in fact, die the following year, and Hyde soon began to wonder about his tale of the mine. He was familiar with the reservation and knew the various landmarks that Duckett had described to him. He also had some experience in mining and so was certain that he could locate the silver. However, Hyde himself suddenly fell ill and died just a short time later. With his passing the last knowledge of the critical location was seemingly lost.[16]

However, according to the Hyde family, part of what Duckett had told Ray Hyde was that the Navajo silver mine was in the "third toe of the turkey track."[17] This enigmatic description may possibly have referred to a branching canyon, perhaps a main canyon with two tributaries coming in close together on either side. Seen from above, this arrangement would, indeed, resemble the shape of a turkey's footprint. Based on the location of Joe Duckett's later searches, this "third toe" canyon may have been a western tributary of today's Piute Canyon.

Piute Canyon extends from the Tall Mountain area to the San Juan River just east of Navajo Mountain. That it may, in fact, be a key geographical point, seems to be confirmed in a statement by David C. Lowry. Lowry owned and operated Vermilion Cliffs Lodge, just off of the Navajo reservation in northern Arizona, from 1929 until 1937. Without mentioning any source, he later stated that the Myrick and Mitchell strike was in Piute Canyon.[18]

In an article printed in 1947, Neil Clark, who received the information from longtime Monument Valley trading post operator Harry Goulding, told the following story. According to Goulding, sometime in the 1930s, during the Great Depression, he became acquainted with an elderly Navajo who was said to be the last survivor of the six tribesmen who had finally buried and hidden the Pish-la-ki mine. Now, in the present economic crisis, the old man and his family were in dire straits. Though reluctant to do so, he was finally convinced by Goulding to go to the mine and take out just enough valuable ore to help him and his close relatives.

The Navajo had hardly left on this venture, however, when a cold and soaking three-day rain set in. The old man got sick, could not go on any farther, and was barely able to make it back to the trading post. His misfortune, he insisted, was due to the gods' displeasure at his starting for the mine. He had had enough and could not be persuaded to try again.[19]

The above story seems to have some similar connotations with one told by former Piute Mesa resident Willie Grayeyes. He remembers that around the 1930s the one or two remaining Navajo elders were urged by some of the younger men to divulge the location of the Pish-la-ki mine. They insisted that it could be developed and its rich resources utilized by the Navajo Mountain community. However, the elders prevailed and the location of the silver continued to remain a secret.[20]

In the summer of 1944, Preston "Pep" Redd and his father, Charles Redd, drove south from their home in Blanding, Utah, to visit John Wetherill at his trading post home in Kayenta. Their stated purpose was to have him show them the location of the old Myrick-Mitchell mine.

However, when they got there, Wetherill was confined to his bed with what was said to be a bad heart. He, obviously, could not take them at that time, but promised to do so as soon as he felt better. However, like many a "lost mine" tale, and what purportedly happened in several prior Pish-la-ki accounts, Wetherill passed away just a few short months later without ever having a chance to take the Redds to the mine site.[21] Just why the Redds believed that Wetherill could take them to the legendary mine, when he himself had searched unsuccessfully for it for so many years, is not explained.

The latter half of the 1900s, as far as is known, evidenced no new searches for the Pish-la-ki mine. Geologic studies done in the middle part of the century had indicated no valuable mineral resources in the Monument Valley-Navajo Mountain region other than copper, and then later on, uranium. There, of course, could be no monetary gain in the finding of the mine at any rate, as it would be located within the boundaries of the Navajo Nation reservation. The Myrick and Mitchell mine, for all intents and purposes, now become simply a legend.

*   *   *

An incident, however, in the new millennium of the 2000s, does bring to mind one additional page that is perhaps connected to the silver mine story. In 2007, Navajo guide Leo Manheimer was leading a hiking group across the plateau-land between Kaibito Creek and the southern rim of Navajo Canyon. Near the canyon he noticed a rectangular slab of rock that stood upright between two supporting piles of rocks. It had obviously been intentionally placed there. Some ninety feet away, down a slope of broken rock, were then seen two small stone cairns. It was quickly learned that if a person sighted from the rock slab directly between the two cairns, a somewhat isolated sandstone dome could be seen beyond that rose some sixty feet above the surrounding ground. Manheimer said that this odd combination of features reminded him of a story that he had heard while growing up in the Navajo Canyon area.

According to this tale, back in the 1800s a group of Navajo had spotted three Anglo (white) prospectors heading east. During a chase that lasted several days and covered many miles, the prospectors were eventually overtaken and, one by one, killed. Although their bags held no ore of any kind, the Navajos did find a map on the body of the last man. It showed a landscape in some detail that looked, in Manheimer's recollection of the account, much like the one the present hiking group was traversing.

Maybe, the modern-day hikers surmised, the desperate prospectors had cached any valuable ore they may have had during the days-long pursuit. Perhaps they had left this distinctively-shaped rock to mark that location. Manheimer and his group then spent some time searching around the sandstone knob and looking into its eroded nooks and crannies, but ultimately found nothing.[22]

This story is reminiscent of one printed in *Arizona Highways* magazine back in 1953. In that account, long before the turn of the century two prospectors, whom the Navajos called Redbeard and Little Gray Fox, were camped near the foot of Navajo Mountain. For whatever reason there was an argument of some sort, and Redbeard severely injured three of the local *Diné*. Gathering reinforcements, the vengeful Navajos started in pursuit of the two white men, who had fled into the rough canyons to the south. At sundown a pitched battle ensued, with Redbeard finally being killed. But Little Gray Fox escaped once more.

The rest of the story, as told years later by a descendant of one of the pursuing Navajos, is a complicated affair having to do with the intricate route left by Little Gray Fox as he fled west into the maze of canyons. For two days and nights the *Diné* braves trailed him, sometimes just a short way behind, but they never caught up with him. After leaving a trail made up of a series of interlocking ovals, the wily prospector finally slipped out to the river, crossed it, and made good his escape.[23]

The "maze of canyons" was undoubtedly Navajo Canyon and its various tributaries, while the "river" that the fleeing prospector ultimately crossed to safety would have been the Colorado. This, indeed, would have been the exact country crossed years later by the hiking group led by Leo Manheimer.

John Wetherill, Ca. 1910-15
Courtesy of Harvey Leake, Wetherill Collection

Louisa Wetherill, Ca. 1910-15
Courtesy of Harvey Leake, Wetherill Collection

Old prospector and burros Navajo Mountain Trading Post, mid-1930's
Courtesy of Madelene Dunn Cameron

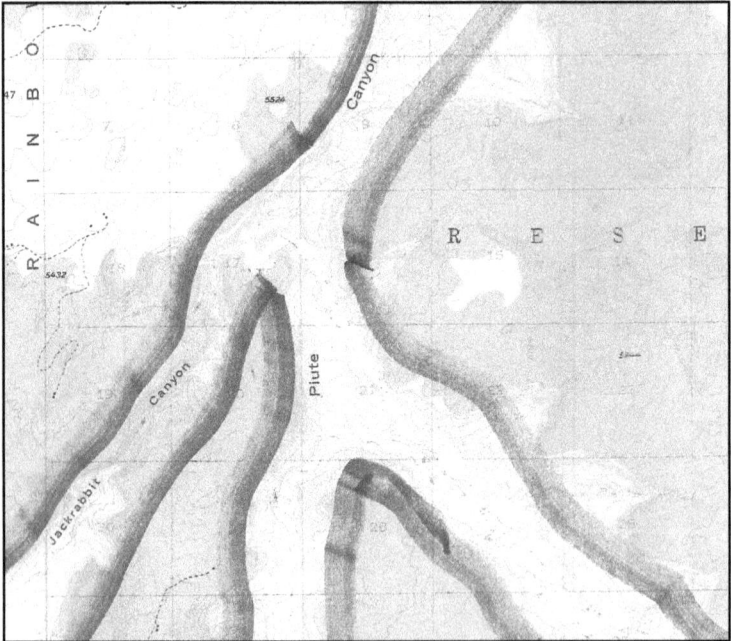

The "turkey track" Piute Canyon
U.S. Geological Survey quadrangle map

Navajo "prospector" petroglyph
Navajo Canyon area

Conclusion

Two important questions, of course, still remain unanswered about the Lost Myrick and Mitchell Silver Mine. Is, or was there, in fact, a Pish-la-ki Mine of the Navajos? And, if so, just where is, or was, it located?

As for the actual existence of the mine, we must rely on the 1939 statements of Hashkéneinii Biyé. As far as is known, his is the only first-hand account of it being found by his father sometime in the months following the *Diné* escape from U.S. troops in 1864. Ever since the Spanish expeditions into what is now the American Southwest in the 16th century, Native Americans have often told the inquisitive white man "what he wanted to hear." In most cases this was to keep him moving on and out of the immediate territory of the natives. However, Hashkéneinii Biyé had no such reason to mislead his interviewer. If so, he would have undoubtedly strongly denied any existence of such a mine. But instead, he readily admitted its longtime presence and use by his father's band.

Therefore, the Pish-la-ki mine most probably was an actual location. The Navajos of Hashkéneinii's domain did, in fact, have an abundance of silver for their various ornaments. And finally, American prospectors did find samples of smelted silver ore at different places in the region.

If, then, there indeed was a Myrick and Mitchell mine, just where was it located? As time passed and various prospecting expeditions searched for the mine, its location was often described, especially in later years, as being somewhere in the Monument Valley area. This belief was most likely based on the fact that the two prospectors, Myrick and Mitchell, were killed there. Added to this may have been the various accounts which placed sacks of silver ore with, or near, the slain bodies.

While it is scientifically true that igneous intrusions are often host to most metallic ores, and several of these bodies do in fact dot the Monument Valley landscape, the only metallic minerals found there have been copper in the 1880s and 1890s, and uranium in the 1950s and 1960s. This has been confirmed by geological studies and surveys carried out by both governmental and private concerns in the 1930s and 1950s. But most important, historically speaking at least, nowhere was it ever stated that the unlucky prospectors actually obtained their silver in the valley of monuments – merely that they were camped and killed there.

Some of the early accounts of the Myrick and Mitchell mine place it in one of the deep canyons that surround Navajo Mountain. East, West, and Lake Canyons (present-day Piute, Navajo, and Tsegi Canyons) were all named at one time or another. However, this was very probably from the finding in each of these sandstone gorges so-called rock smelters with fragments of silver ore, and even small buttons of nearly pure silver, scattered around them. Significantly, though, the source of this silver – the mine itself – was not found at any of these sites, just the workings from its ore.

Therefore, for the actual location of the Pish-la-ki mine, we must once again rely on the words of Hashkéneinii Biyé. He specifically stated that his father found the outcrop of silver "on Navajo Mountain." Geologically speaking, this makes perfect sense. The mountain is an igneous intrusion from below known as a laccolith. In the far distant past an upwelling of molten magma pushed its way upwards from deep beneath the Earth's surface. It did not, however, force its way out in the form of a volcanic eruption, though it did push and arch upwards the overlying sedimentary rock strata into a blister-like dome almost four thousand feet high. The early mining men were correct in their belief that precious metals such as gold and silver originate in and are then precipitated out from magma far below ground level. If such cooled and solidified igneous bodies were eventually exposed at the surface by erosion, then hopefully, the gold or silver ore they might contain could be extracted by various mining methods. However, the Navajo Mountain laccolith has not been revealed by the erasers of time and nature.

In some instances, though, valuable metals can reach the surface by another means. If groundwater, seeping deep down into the Earth's crust by way of cracks and fissures in the rock, approaches near enough to the extremely high temperatures of a molten magma body, it can dissolve and concentrate metallic elements such as silver. Then, when this superheated water, because of its lower density, eventually begins to make its way back up toward the surface, the elemental silver often starts to combine with sulphur or chlorine elements to form compounds. As the temperature of these hydrothermal fluids begins to cool, the minerals argentite and chlorargyrite start to form. These, then, can finally reach the surface and be deposited as silver ores. The mineral chlorargyrite, sometimes known as "horn silver," is most often found in dry, desert-like conditions.

The Navajo Mountain area is just such a locale. When the magma pushed upwards, the overlying rock layers were bent and stretched, with the solid stone finally breaking and cracking. One of these resulting fractures could have provided an ideal conduit for rising hydrothermal fluids and their precious cargo of silver. When in 1882 prospector M.S. Foote registered disappointment in only finding sedimentary sandstone rock exposed on Navajo Mountain, he was evidently unaware of the possibility of silver ore being exposed through one of these cracks.

Contemporary accounts in the early 1880s that describe the movements of Charles Myrick and Hernan Mitchell have them crossing the plateau on the west before dropping down into Monument Valley and their eventual fate. There is a long-used Native American trail that leads from the western part of the valley, in the area of Agathla Peak, up the talus slope known as The Ramp, to the top of Hoskaninni Mesa. Travelers along this route could then continue westward, skirting the head of Nokai Canyon and traversing the upper portion of Piute Canyon. This path would eventually bring them to Navajo Mountain.

Both Paiute and Navajo sources say that the two prospectors were followed anywhere from one to three days before they descended back down into Monument Valley. This would have been an adequate amount of time for them to have come from the Navajo Mountain area and to eventually meet their demise among the buttes of Monument Valley. Indeed, they did not have even been clear to the mountain itself. Myrick himself said that he had originally found his specimens of silver ore in the vicinity of three old smelters, probably in one of the nearby canyons.

Therefore, there very well could have been an outcropping of silver somewhere on Navajo Mountain, its so-called "ledges" being the narrow, exposed opening of one of the rock fissures that eons ago carried silver-rich hydrothermal fluids to the surface. Even if the Navajo stories of its eventual concealment are just that, stories, the finding of such an outcrop would still be like that of the proverbial "needle in a haystack." The exact site of the Pish-la-ki mine of the *Diné* on Navajo Mountain remains hidden, either by the hand of nature or that of man. And the legend of the Myrick and Mitchell mine, too, remains just that – an intriguing and enticing legend.

Light-colored sedimentary sandstone encircling base of Navajo Mountain

Maps

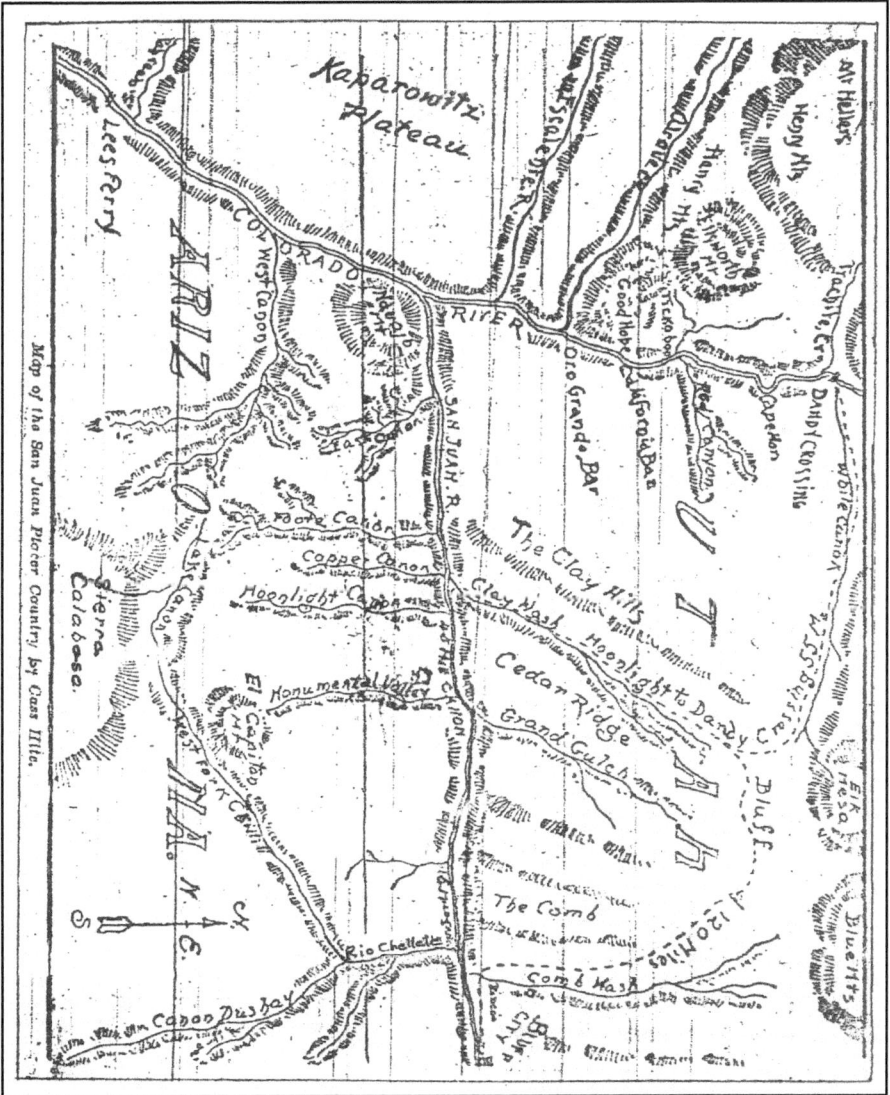

Map of the San Juan Placer Country
By Cass Hite Denver News, 8 January 1893

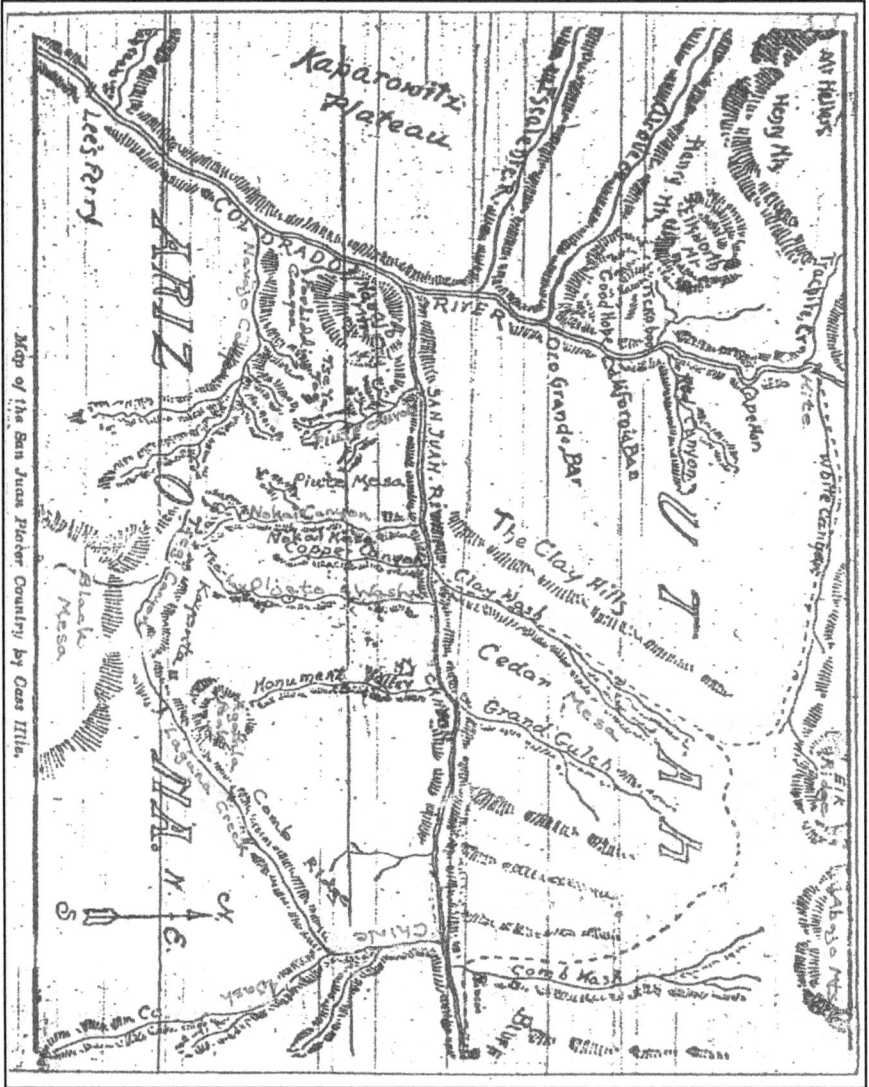

Cass Hite 1893 map with modern names

Endnotes

Chapter One:

1. Charles Kelly. "Chief Hoskaninni." From notes of April, 1939 interview. Charles Kelly Papers. Utah State Historical Society, Salt Lake City. 3-4.

2. Byron Cummings. *Indians I Have Known.* Tucson: Arizona Silhouettes, 1952. 2-3.
Also, Richard E. Klinck. *The Land of Room Enough and Time Enough.* Albuquerque: University of New Mexico Press, 1953. 24-25.

3. Kelly. "Chief Hoskaninni." 4.

4. Ibid. 5.

5. Cy Warman. "The Peso-la-ki Mine." *Denver Republican.* July 18, 1897. 28.

6. Ssac [Cass Hite]. "Peso-La-Ki!" *The Southwest* (Durango, Colorado). May 5, 1883. 1.

Chapter Two:

1. H.L. Mitchell. Letter, December 24, 1879. Letters Received, Office of Indian Affairs, New Mexico Superintendency, 1879. Record Group 75. Washington, D.C.: National Archives and Records Administration.

2. H.L. Mitchell. Letters, February 5 and February 15, 1880.

3. "Editorial and Otherwise." *Dolores News* (Rico, Colorado). February 21, 1880. 1.

4. C. Gregory Crampton. *Outline History of the Glen Canyon Region, 1776 to 1922.* University of Utah Anthropological Papers No. 42. Salt Lake City: University of Utah Press, 1959.

5. David E. Miller. *Hole-in-the-Rock: An Epic in the Colonization of the Great American West.* Salt Lake City: University of Utah Press, 1959. 90.

6. J.Y. Carpenter. Letter to C. Shurtz, Department of Interior. February 28, 1880.
   Ssac [Cass Hite]. "Peso-La-Ki!" *The Southwest* (Durango, Colorado). May 5, 1883. 1.

7. George P. Schurtz. Letter to Charles Kelly. July 26, 1940. Charles Kelly Papers. Utah State Historical Society, Salt Lake City.
   Austin and Alta Fife. "Interview: Mrs. Billie Nevills. July 28, 1946." Fife Mormon Collections. Collection I: Oral Sources. 501.

8. Ssac [Cass Hite]. "The Peso-La-Ki!" *The Southwest* (Durango, Colorado). May 5, 1883. 1.

9. Edith L. Watson. "Golden Phantoms." *The Pueblo* (Colorado) *Indicator.* September 14, 1935. 3.
   Randall Henderson. "Navajo Gods Guard the Silver of Pish-la-ki." *Desert Magazine.* December, 1950. 5.

10. Richard E. Klinck. *Land of Room Enough and Time Enough.* Albuquerque: University of New Mexico Press, 1959. 27-28.

11. "Murder." *Dolores News* (Rico, Colorado). March 13, 1880. 1.

12. "Peso-La-Ki!" *The Southwest* (Durango, Colorado). May 5, 1883. 1.

13. "Ledges of Mineral." *The Rocky Mountain News* (Denver, Colorado). December 30, 1892. 1.

14. James M. Rush, Jr. *Great Sage Plain to Timberline: Our Pioneer History.* Volume IV. Cortez, Colorado: Montezuma County Historical Society, 2009. 59.

15. John R. Winslowe. "Gold Canyon." *True West.* July-August, 1966. 7.

16. Arthur H. Spencer. "Lost Silver Mine of Monumental Valley." Unpub. mss. Otis R. "Dock" Marston Papers. Box 369, folder 19. The Huntington Library. San Marino, California.

17. "Indian Imps." *Denver Tribune*. March 16, 1880. 1.

18. "New Mineral Excitement." *The Durango* (Colorado) *Record*. January 20, 1882. 4.

19. H.L. Mitchell. Letter, December 24, 1879.

20. "Tax List." *The Durango* (Colorado) *Herald*. August 31, 1883. 7.

21. U.S. Bureau of the Census. "1880 Federal Census for State of Colorado."

22. "New Mineral Excitement." 4.

23. "Ledges of Mineral." *Rocky Mountain News* (Denver, Colorado). December 30, 1892. 1.

24. David E. Miller. *Hole-in-the-Rock*. 92.

25. "An Armed Expedition." *Dolores News* (Rico, Colorado). September 18, 1880. 1.

Chapter Three:

1. C.A. Frost. Letter to Otis Marston. December 20, 1960. Otis R. "Dock" Marston Collection. Box 369, folder 19. The Huntington Library. San Marino, California.

2. C. Alfred Frost. *Rattlesnakes & Wild Horses and Other Campfire Tales*. No city: River Road Press, 1993. 54.

3. No title. *Mancos* (Colorado) *Times*. February 25, 1898. 1.

4. Frances Gillmor and Louisa Wade Wetherill. *Traders to the Navajos: The Story of the Wetherills of Kayenta*. Boston: Houghton Mifflin Company, 1934. 17.

5. Montezuma County Historical Society. *Great Sage Plain to Timberline: Our Pioneer History*. Cortez, Colorado: Montezuma County Historical Society, 2009. 59.

6. A.H. Spencer. "Lost Silver Mine of Monumental Valley." Otis R. "Dock" Marston Papers. Box 369, folder 19. The Huntington Library. San Marino, California.

7. Austin and Alta Fife. *Saints of Sage and Saddle: Folklore Among the Mormons*. Bloomington: University of Indiana Press, 1956. 288-89.

8. Morgan Monroe. "Indian Country Trek." *Desert Magazine*. August, 1949. 28.

9. Pearl Baker. *Trail on the Water*. Boulder, Colorado: Pruett Publishing Company, no date (ca 1969). 62.

10. "One of the Hites." *Rocky Mountain News* (Denver, Colorado). January 13, 1893. 12.

11. Richard E. Klinck. *Land of Room Enough and Time Enough*. Albuquerque: University of New Mexico Press, 1953. 29.

12. "Silver Mine Still Lost, Or Is It?" *Four Corners* (Dolores, Colorado). Vol. 1, 1959. 1.

13. "Many Have Been Killed." *Durango* (Colorado) *Herald*. January 5, 1893. 4.

14. Ibid.

15. Austin and Alta Fife. 288-89.

16. C. Alfred Frost. 54-55.

17. David E. Miller. *Hole-in-the-Rock: An Epic in the Colonization of the Great American West*. Salt Lake City: University of Utah Press, 1959. 90.

Chapter Four:

1. David E. Miller. *Hole-in-the-Rock: An Epic in the Colonization of the Great American West*. Salt Lake City: University of Utah Press, 1959. 90-91.

2. Ibid. 91-92.

3. Austin and Alta Fife. *Saints of Sage and Saddle: Folklore Among the Mormons*. Bloomington: University of Indiana Press, 1956. 289-90.

4. Frances Gillmor and Louisa Wade Wetherill. *Traders to the Navajo: The Story of the Wetherills of Kayenta*. Boston: Houghton Mifflin Company, 1934. 95-96.

5. J. Ferrell Colton. *My Arizona*. Privately printed, 2002. 112.

6. Charles Kelly. "Chief Hoskaninni." From notes of April, 1939 interview. Charles Kelly Papers. Utah State Historical Society, Salt Lake City. 8-9.

7. A.H. Spencer. "Lost Silver Mine of Monumental Valley." Unpub. mss. Otis R. "Dock" Marston Collection. Box 369, folder19. The Huntington Library. San Marino, California.

8. Austin and Alta Fife. Ibid.
   Richard E. Klinck. *Land of Room Enough and Time Enough*. Albuquerque: University of New Mexico Press, 1953. 30.

9. Galen Eastman. Letter to Commissioner of Indian Affairs, Washington, D.C. February 6, 1880.

10. Captain F.T. Bennett. Letter to Assistant Adjutant General, Department of New Mexico, Santa Fe. March 22, 1880.

11. H.L. Mitchell. Letter to Lt. Col. R.E.A. Crofton, Post Commander, Fort Lewis, Colorado. June 21, 1881."

12. Albert R. Lyman. "The Fort on the Firing Line." *The Improvement Era*. October, 1949. 639.

13. Albert R. Lyman. *The Outlaw of Navaho Mountain*. Salt Lake City: Deseret Book Company, 1963. 14-22.

14. A.H. Spencer. Ibid.

15. Laura Graves. *Thomas Varker Keam, Indian Trader*. Norman: University of Oklahoma Press, 1998. 101-03.

16. Alexander M. Stephen. Deposition. August 17, 1882. Keam's Canyon, Arizona Territory.

17. William Ross. Deposition. August 3, 1882. Fort Defiance, Arizona Territory.

18. Jonathan P. Williams. Deposition. August 4, 1882. Territory of Arizona.

Chapter Five:

1. "Many Have Been Killed." *Durango* (Colorado) *Herald*. January 5, 1893. 4.

2. "Ledges of Mineral." *Rocky Mountain News* (Denver, Colorado). December 30, 1892. 1.

3. "Killed by Indians." *Rocky Mountain News* (Denver, Colorado). March 16, 1880. 8.
"Interesting Career of Indian Scout, Pioneer Cattleman, Comes to a Close." *Times-Independent* (Moab, Utah). May 31, 1934. 8.

4. "Indian Imps." *Denver Tribune*. March 16, 1880. 1.

5. H.L. Mitchell. Letter to Col. Henry J. Page, U.S. Indian Agent, Ignacio, Colorado. February 5, 1880.

6. Ibid. February 15, 1880.

7. "Indian Imps." Ibid.

8. George P. Schurtz. Letter to Charles Kelly. July 26, 1940. Charles Kelly Papers. Utah State Historical Society, Salt Lake City.

9. "Interesting Career... Comes to Close." Ibid.
No title. *Mancos* (Colorado) *Times*. April 6, 1894. 1.

10. "Indian Imps." Ibid.

11. H.L. Mitchell. Letter, February 15, 1880. Ibid.

12. Albert R. Lyman. "The Old Settler." *San Juan Record* (Monticello, Utah). July 9, 1953. 1.

Richard E. Klinck. *Land of Room Enough and Time Enough*. Albuquerque: University of New Mexico Press, 1953. 31.

13. J.Y. Carpenter. Letter to Mr. Carl Shurtz, Secretary of the Interior, Washington, D.C. February 28,1880.

14. Ibid.

15. "Murder." *Dolores News Extra* (Rico, Colorado). March 7, 1880. 1.

16. Ibid.

17. "Killed by Indians." Ibid.

18. "Indian Imps." Ibid.

19. "Ledges of Mineral." Ibid.

20. "Interesting Career…." Ibid.

21. George P. Schurtz. Ibid.

22. No title. *The Southwest* (Durango, Colorado). October 25, 1883. 4.

23. No title. *Mancos* (Colorado) *Times*. Ibid.

24. Marion Wetherill. Letter to Alice Brown. March 14, 1910. Copy of letter in author's possession.

25. Pearl Baker. *Trail on the Water*. Boulder, Colorado: Pruett Publishing Company, no date [ca 1969]. 62.

26. Bert Loper. "Notes on Cass Hite. February 4, 1933." Charles Kelly Papers. Utah State Historical Society, Salt Lake City.

27. "Killed by Indians." Ibid.

28. "Ledges of Mineral." Ibid.

29. "The Merrick Gold Mine." *Salt Lake Herald*. April 18, 1897. 3.

Chapter Six:

1. "Local Brevities." *Dolores News* (Rico, Colorado). January 10, 1880. 2.

2. "Murder." *Dolores News Extra*. March 7, 1880. 1.

3. "Our Boys Home Again." *Dolores News*. March 13, 1880. 2.

4. "An Armed Expedition." *Dolores News*. September 18, 1880. 1.

5. "Onward March!" *Dolores News*. October 9, 1880. 4.

6. Frances Gillmor and Louisa Wade Wetherill. *Traders to the Navajo: The Story of the Wetherills of Kayenta*. Boston: Houghton Mifflin Company, 1934. 17-18.

7. Herbert E. Gregory. "Book III, Moki-Navajo, 1910." Field notes, entry for August 5.
    "Book XI, Navajo-Moki, 1914." Field notes, entry for August 28. U.S. Geological Survey Library. Denver, Colorado.

8. Arthur H. Spencer. "Lost Silver Mine of Monumental Valley." Unpub. mss. Otis R. "Dock" Marston Collection. Box 369, folder 19. The Huntington Library. San Marino, California.

9. Gillmor and Wetherill. Ibid. 18.

10. Alexander M. Stephen. "Deposition. August 17, 1882." Keams Canyon, Arizona.

11. "Too Fine to Save." *Rocky Mountain News* (Denver, Colorado). December 23, 1892. 8.

12. No title. *Dolores News* (Rico, Colorado). November 12, 1881. 3.

13. "In Search of Minerals." *Dolores News*. November 19, 1881. 2.

14. Cass Hite. "The Trail of Sixty Snows." Unpub. mss. Charles Kelly Papers. Utah State Historical Society, Salt Lake City.

15. "Cass Hite on the San Juan." *Salt Lake Tribune*. January 12, 1893. 8.

16. "New Mineral Excitement." *Durango* (Colorado) *Record*. January 20, 1882. 4.

17. "New Mineral Excitement" (Continued.) *Durango Record*. January 21, 1882. 4.

18. "The Navajo Mountain Explorers." *Dolores News*. January 28, 1882. 1.

19. "New Mineral Excitement." January 20. Ibid.

Chapter Seven:

1. "Personal." *Durango* (Colorado) *Herald.* January 20, 1882. 3. "Gone to the Navajo Mountain." *Durango* (Colorado) *Record.* January 24, 1882. 4.

2. Ibid.

3. "The Latest from the Navajo Mountain Explorers." *Durango Record.* February 8, 1882. 8.

4. Ibid.

5. "The Navajo Expedition." *Durango Record.* March 31, 1882. 1.

6. Ibid.

7. "San Juan Gold Fields." *Denver Republican.* January 8, 1893. 2.

8. "The Navajo Expedition." Ibid.

9. "Nothing of Note Comes from Navajo Mountain." *Rocky Mountain News* (Denver, Colorado). April 3, 1882. 2.

10. Ibid.

11. "The Navajo Expedition." Ibid.

12. "Another Song Sung by Navajo Explorers." *Rocky Mountain News* (Denver, Colorado). April 14, 1882. 2.

13. Ibid.

Chapter Eight:

1. James H. Knipmeyer. *Cass Hite: The Life of an Old Prospector.* Salt Lake City: University of Utah Press, 2016.

2. "The Great Myrick-Mitchell Mine Reportedly Found." *Durango Record.* March 16, 1882. 4.

3. "A Prospecting Party Goes to Monumental Valley." *Rocky Mountain News* (Denver, Colorado). May 23, 1882. 2.

4. Ibid.

5. Cass Hite. Letter to U.S. Indian Agent Galen Eastman. April 17, 1883. Fort Defiance, Arizona Territory.

6. C. H. [Cass Hite]. "The Copper Canon Country." *Durango* (Colorado) *Herald.* November 3, 1882. 2.

7. Ibid. November 7, 1882. 2.

8. "Way Down Upon the San Juan River." *Salt Lake Herald.* December 16, 1882. 5.

9. C. H. November 5, 1882. 2.

10. James Martin Rush, Jr. Interview. July 17, 1943. Dolores, Colorado. In *Great Sage Plain to Timberline: Our Pioneer History.* Cortez, Colorado: Montezuma County Historical Society, 2009. 59-61.

11. "From the Mancos." *The Southwest* (Durango, Colorado). March 3, 1883. 3.

12. Copper [Cass Hite]. "Utah." *The Southwest.* June 9, 1883. 3.

13. A. H. Spencer. "Lost Silver Mine of Monumental Valley." Unpub. mss. Otis R. "Dock" Marston Collection. Box 369, folder 19. The Huntington Library. San Marino, California.

14. Cy Warman. *Frontier Stories.* New York: Charles Scribner's Sons, 1898. 149-55.

15. Pearl Baker. *Trail on the Water.* Boulder, Colorado: Pruett Publishing Company, no date [1969]. 62-64.

16. Charles Kelly. "Hoskaninni." Unpub. mss. Charles Kelly Papers. Utah State Historical Society, Salt Lake City. 9.

17. "From the Wilderness." *Denver Republican.* August 12, 1889. 1.

18. James W. Black. "Statement of …. July 10, 1930." Flagstaff, Arizona. Gladwell "Toney" Richardson Collection. Special Collections, Cline Library. Northern Arizona University, Flagstaff. 4.

19. Mrs. White Mountain Smith. "Navajo Gold." *Desert Magazine.* November, 1938. 6.

Chapter Nine:

1. Philip Zoeller. Deposition. June 20, 1882. Fort Defiance, Arizona.

2. A.M. Stephen. Deposition. August 17, 1882. Keam's Canyon, Arizona.

3. James R. Sutherland. Deposition. May 1, 1882. Fort Defiance, Arizona.

4. Billie Williams Yost. *Bread Upon the Sands.* Caldwell, Idaho: The Caxton Publishers, Ltd., 1958. 18-19. Also *Diamonds in the Desert.* Flagstaff, Arizona: Silver Spruce Publishing, 1987. 82.

5. Elizabeth Rigby. "Blue Canyon." *Arizona Highways.* August, 1959. 37.

6. "Explorers." *Dolores News* (Rico, Colorado). June 3, 1882. 1.

7. William A. Ross. "Deposition. August 3, 1882." Fort Defiance, Arizona.

8. Jonathan P. Williams. "Deposition. August 4, 1882." Fort Defiance, Arizona.

9. Ssac [Cass Hite]. "Peso-la-ki!" *The Southwest* (Durango, Colorado). May 5, 1883. 1.

10. Ibid.

11. "Pech-La-Ki." *Durango* (Colorado) *Herald.* May 18, 1883. 1.

12. "A Cave of Gold." *The Southwest.* December 1, 1883. 2.

13. Charles L. Bernheimer. "Field Notes, 1927 Expedition." Utah State Historical Society, Salt Lake City. 121.

14. J. Lee Correll. "Trouble in Monument Valley." *Utah Historical Quarterly.* Spring, 1971. 151-52.

15. Victor E. Neff. Statement of .... September 6, 1887. Ignacio, Southern Ute Reservation.

16. Betty Robertson Kaufman. *Henry L. Mitchell of Missouri ... and the Lower San Juan River*. Denver: Kaufman Publishing, 2006. 80.

17. J. Lee Correll. Ibid.

18. Robert S. McPherson. "Murder in the Land of Death: The Walcott-McNally Incident." *Utah Historical Quarterly*. Summer, 2013. 249-66.

19. Leo Manheimer. Personal communication to author. May 9, 2019. Navajo Mountain, Utah.

20. William F. Williams. Statement of .... May 22, 1929. Winslow, Arizona. Gladwell "Tony" Richardson Collection. Special Collections, Cline Library. University of Northern Arizona, Flagstaff.

21. Gladwell Richardson. *Indian Trader*. Tucson: University of Arizona Press, 1986. 87.

22. E.J. Johnson. "Navajo Indians Murder Prospectors Who Refuse to Stay Away from Mine." *The Arizona Republic* (Phoenix). April 14, 1926. Sec. 2, p. 1.

23. Gladwell Richardson. Ibid.

24. Heber Christensen. Letter to Frank Beckwith, June 6, 1934. Charles Kelly Papers. Utah State Historical Society. Salt Lake City.

Chapter Ten:

1. James H. Knipmeyer. *Joe Duckett: The Hermit of Montezuma Canyon*. Chula Vista, California: Aventine Press, 2011. 5, 15-16.

2. Ibid. 20.

3. Thad Duckett. "Diary: 1890-91." Photocopy in author's possession. Also, James Curtis. *Riding Old Trails*. Grand Junction, Colorado: Country Press, 1976. 197-208.

4. Winn Westcott. Personal interview with author. September 22, 2005. Monticello, Utah.

5. C. Alfred Frost. *Rattlesnakes & Wild Horses and Other Campfire Tales*. No city: River Road Press, 1993. 59-60.

6. Hilda Faunce. *Desert Wife*. Boston: Little, Brown and Company, 1934. 251-63.

7. "Local Brevities." *The Coconino Sun* (Flagstaff, Arizona). June 30, 1892. 3.

8. John Upton Terrell. "Desert Folk Believe Ruess Killer Victim." *Salt Lake Tribune*. August 28, 1935. 1.

9. "Mining Claims, Miscellaneous Book A. January 1, 1891 to May 16, 1894." San Juan County Courthouse. Monticello, Utah. 23-26.

10. C. A. Frost. Letter to Mr. Otis Marston. December 20, 1960. Otis R. "Dock" Marston Collection. Box 369, folder 19. The Huntington Library. San Marino, California.

11. James W. Black. "Statement of .... July 10, 1930." Flagstaff, Arizona. Special Collections, Cline Library. University of Northern Arizona, Flagstaff.

12. Herbert E. Gregory. "Field Notes. Navajo-Moki Book VIII (1913). U. S. Geological Survey Library. Denver, Colorado.

13. Kathryn Gabriel. *Marietta Wetherill: Reflections on Life with the Navajos in Chaco Canyon*. Boulder, Colorado: Johnson Books, 1992. 51, 55.

14. "The Merrick Gold Mine." *Salt Lake Herald*. April 18, 1897. 3.

Chapter Eleven:

1. John Wetherill. Testimony in River Bed Case, 1929-30. 1626-29.

2. Frances Gillmor and Louisa Wade Wetherill. *Traders to the Navajos: The Story of the Wetherills of Kayenta*. Boston: Houghton Mifflin Company, 1934. 59-60.

3. Richard Van Valkenburgh. "Monument Valley." *Arizona Highways*. April, 1940. 14.

4. Francis J. Dyer. "Adventures in a Land of Wonders." *Overland Monthly*. October, 1911. 344-46.

5. Dolph and Irene Andrus. *The Life Story of Dolph and Irene Andrus and Their Family: The Bluff Years 1915-1918*. Sunland, California: Privately printed, 1967. 24.

6. Muriel Pope. Letter to Otis R. Marston. December 16, 1956. Otis R. "Dock" Marston Collection. Box 369, folder 19. The Huntington Library. San Marino, California.

7. W. T. Shelton. Letter to John Wetherill. October 19, 1906. Otis R. "Dock" Marston Collection. Box 369, folder, 19. The Huntington Library. San Marino, California.

8. Harvey Leake. Personal communication to the author. September, 2017.

9. A. H. Spencer. "Lost Silver of Monumental Valley." Unpub. mss. Otis R. "Dock" Marston Collection. Box 369, folder 19. The Huntington Library. San Marino, California. 1.

10. Ibid. 2.

11. Hilda Faunce. *Desert Wife*. Boston: Little, Brown and Company, 1934. 265-75.

12. C. Alfred Frost. *Rattlesnakes & Wild Horses and Other Campfire Tales*. No city: River Road Press, 1993. 61-63.

13. Madelene Dunn Cameron. Personal interview with author. June 7, 1996. Miami, Oklahoma.

14. Gladwell Richardson. *Navajo Trader*. Tucson: University of Arizona Press, 1986. 43.

15. Gillmor and Wetherill. 236.

16. C. Alfred Frost. 59-60.

17. Winn Westcott. Personal interview with author. September 22, 2005. Monticello, Utah.

18. David C. Lowry. Letter to Otis R. Marston. February 2, 1959. Otis R. "Dock" Marston Collection. Box 369, folder 19. The Huntington Library. San Marino, California.

19. Neil M. Clark. "Desert Trader." *Saturday Evening Post*. March 29, 1947. 117.

20. Leo Manheimer. Personal communication to author. May 9, 2019. Navajo Mountain, Utah.

21. Preston Redd. *From Horseback to Cadillac, I'm Still a Cowboy*. Tempe, Arizona: Tavas Cash Press, 1988. 229-30.

22. Luke Dittrich. "Over the Rainbow." *Backpacker*. December, 2007. 28-29.

23. Cecil Calvin Richardson. "The Lost Legion of Wanderers." *Arizona Highways*. August, 1953. 13-14.

Bibliography

Andrus, Dolph and Irene. *The Life Story of... and Their Family: The Bluff Years. 1915-1918.* Sunland, California: Privately printed, 1967.

Baker, Pearl. *Travel on the Water.* Boulder, Colorado: Pruett Publishing Company, no date (ca 1969).

Bennett, Captain F. T. Letter to Assistant Adjutant General, Department of New Mexico, Santa Fe. March 22, 1880. Letters Received, Record Group 75. National Archives And Records Administration. Washington, D.C.

Bernheimer, Charles L. "Field Notes, 1927 Expedition." Utah State Historical Society. Salt Lake City.

Black, James W. "Statement of...." July 10, 1930. Flagstaff, Arizona. Gladwell "Toney"

Richardson Collection. Special Collections, Cline Library. Northern Arizona University. Flagstaff.

Cameron, Madelene Dunn. Personal interview with author. June 7, 1996. Miami, Oklahoma.

Carpenter, J. Y. Letter to C. Shurtz, Department of Interior. February 28, 1880. Letters Received, Record Group 75. National Archives and Records Administration. Washington, D.C.

Christensen, Heber. Letter to Frank Beckwith, June 6, 1934. Charles Kelly Papers. Utah State Historical Society, Salt Lake City.

Clark, Neil M. "Desert Trader." *Saturday Evening Post.* March 29, 1947.

Coconino Sun (Flagstaff, Arizona). "Local Brevities." June 30, 1892.

Colton, J. Ferrell. *My Arizona.* Privately printed, 2002.

Copper (Cass Hite). "Utah." *The Southwest* (Durango, Colorado). June 9, 1883.

Correll, J. Lee. "Trouble in Monument Valley." *Utah Historical Quarterly*. Spring, 1971.

Crampton, C. Gregory. *Outline History of the Glen Canyon Region, 1776 to 1922*. University of Utah Anthropological Paper No. 42. Salt Lake City: University of Utah Press, 1959.

Cummings, Byron. *Indians I Have Known*. Tucson: Arizona Silhouettes, 1952.

Curtis, James. *Riding Old Trails*. Grand Junction, Colorado: Country Press, 1976.

Denver Republican. "From the Wilderness." August 12, 1889.
"San Juan Gold Fields." January 8, 1893.

Denver Tribune. "Indian Imps." March 16, 1880.

Dittrich, Luke. "Over the Rainbow." *Backpacker*. December, 2007.

Dolores News (Rico, Colorado). "Local Brevities." January 10, 1880.
"Editorial and Otherwise." February 21, 1880.
"Murder." March 13, 1880.
"Our Boys Home Again." March 13, 1880.
"An Armed Expedition." September 18, 1880.
"Onward March!" October 9, 1880.
No title. November 12, 1881.
"In Search of Minerals." November 19, 1881.
"The Navajo Mountain Explorers. January 28, 1882.
"Explorers." June 3, 1882.

Dolores News Extra. "Murder." March 7, 1880.

Duckett, Thad. "Diary: 1890-91." Photocopy in author's possession.

Durango (Colorado) *Herald*. "Personal." January 20, 1882.
"Pech-La-Ki." May 18, 1883.
"Tax List." August 31, 1883.
"Many Have Been Killed." January 5, 1893.

Durango (Colorado) *Record*. "New Mineral Excitement." January 20, 1882.
"Continued." January 21, 1882.
"Gone to the Navajo Mountain." January 24, 1882.

"The Latest from the Navajo Mountain Explorers." February 8, 1882.

"The Great Myrick-Mitchell Mine Reportedly Found." March 16, 1882.

"The Navajo Expedition." March 31, 1882.

Dyer, Francis J. "Adventures in a Land of Wonders." *Overland Monthly.* October, 1911.

Eastman, Galen. Letter to Commissioner of Indian Affairs, Washington, D.C. February 6, 1880.

Letters Received, Record Group 75. National Archives and Records Administration. Washington, D.C.

Faunce, Hilda. *Desert Wife.* Boston: Little, Brown and Company, 1934.

Fife, Austin and Alta. "Interview: Mrs. Billie Nevills. July 28, 1946." Fife Mormon Collections. Collection I: Oral Sources. Utah State University. Logan, Utah.

Four Corners (Dolores, Colorado). "Silver Mine Still Lost, Or Is It?" Volume 1, 1959.

Frost, C. A. Letter to Otis Marston. December 20, 1960. Otis R. "Dock" Marston Papers. Box 369, folder 19. The Huntington Library. San Marino, California.

Frost, C. Alfred. *Rattlesnakes & Wild Horses and Other Campfire Tales.* No city: River Road Press, 1993.

Gabriel, Kathryn. *Marietta Wetherill: Reflections on Life With the Navajos in Chaco Canyon.* Boulder, Colorado: Johnson Books, 1992.

Gillmor, Frances and Louisa Wade Wetherill. *Traders to the Navajos: The Story of the Wetherills of Kayenta.* Boston: Houghton Mifflin Company, 1934.

Graves, Laura. *Thomas Varker Keam: Indian Trader.* Norman: University of Oklahoma Press, 1998.

Gregory, Herbert E. "Book III, Moki-Navajo, 1910." U.S. Geological Survey Library. Denver, Colorado.

"Book VIII, Navajo-Moki, 1913."

"Book XI, Navajo-Moki, 1914."

Henderson, Randall. "Navajo Gods Guard the Silver of Pish-la-ki." *Desert Magazine*. December, 1950.

Hite, Cass. "The Copper Canyon Country." *Durango* (Colorado) *Herald*. November 3, 1882.
"The Copper Canyon Country." *Durango Herald*. November 5, 1882.
"The Copper Canyon Country." *Durango Herald*. November 7, 1882.
Letter to U.S. Indian Agent Galen Eastman. April 17, 1883. Fort Defiance, Arizona.
"The Trail of Sixty Snows." Unpublished manuscript. Charles Kelly Papers. Utah State Historical Society. Salt Lake City.

Johnson, E. J. "Navajo Indians Murder Prospectors Who Refuse to Stay Away from Mine."
The Arizona Republic (Phoenix). April 14, 1926.

Kaufman, Betty Robertson. *Henry L. Mitchell of Missouri... and the Lower San Juan River*. Denver: Kaufman Publishing, 2006.

Kelly, Charles. "Chief Hoskaninni." From notes of April, 1939 interview. Charles Kelly Papers. Utah State Historical Society. Salt Lake City.

Klinck, Richard E. *Land of Room Enough and Time Enough*. Albuquerque: University of New Mexico Press, 1959.

Knipmeyer, James H. *Joe Duckett: The Hermit of Montezuma Canyon*. Chula Vista, California: Aventine Press, 2011.
Cass Hite: The Life of an Old Prospector. Salt Lake City: University of Utah Press, 2016.

Leake, Harvey. Personal communication to author. September, 2017. Prescott, Arizona.

Loper, Bert. "Notes on Cass Hite. February 4, 1933." Charles Kelly Papers. Utah State Historical Society. Salt Lake City.

Lowry, David C. Letter to Otis R. Marston. February 2, 1959. Otis R. "Dock" Marston Papers. Box 369, folder 19. The Huntington Library. San Marino, California.

Lyman, Albert R. "The Fort on the Firing Line." *The Improvement Era.* October, 1949.

"The Old Settler." *San Juan Record* (Monticello, Utah). July 9, 1953.

The Outlaw of Navajo Mountain. Salt Lake City: Deseret Book Company, 1963.

McPherson, Robert F. "Murder in the Land of Death: The Walcott-McNally Incident." *Utah Historical Quarterly.* Summer, 2013.

Mancos (Colorado) *Times.* No title. April 6, 1894.

Manheimer, Leo. Personal communication to author. May 9, 2019. Navajo Mountain, Utah.

Miller, David E. *Hole-in-the-Rock: An Epic in the Colonization of the Great American West.* Salt Lake City: University of Utah Press, 1959.

"Mining Claims, Miscellaneous Book A. January 1, 1891 to May 16, 1894." San Juan County Courthouse. Monticello, Utah.

Mitchell, Henry L. Letter. December 24, 1879. Letters Received, Record Group 75. National Archives and Records Administration. Washington, D.C.

Letter to Col. Henry J. Page, U.S. Indian Agent, Ignacio, Colorado. February 5, 1880.

Letter to Col. Henry J. Page. February 15, 1880.

Letter to Lt. Col. R.E.A. Crofton, Post Commander, Fort Lewis, Colorado. June 21, 1881

Monroe, Morgan. "Indian Country Trek." *Desert Magazine.* August, 1949.

Neff, Victor E. "Statement of September 6, 1887." Ignacio, Southern Ute Reservation.

Pope, Muriel. Letter to Otis R. Marston. December 16, 1956. Otis R. "Dock" Marston

Papers. Box 369, folder 19. The Huntington Library. San Marino, California.

Redd, Preston. *From Horseback to Cadillac: I'm Still a Cowboy.* Tempe, Arizona: Tavas Cash Press, 1988.

Richardson, Cecil Calvin. "The Lost Legion of Wanderers." *Arizona Highways.* August, 1953.

Richardson, Gladwell. *Indian Trader.* Tucson: University of Arizona Press, 1986.

Rigby, Elizabeth. "Blue Canyon." *Arizona Highways.* August, 1959.

Rocky Mountain News (Denver, Colorado). "Nothing of Note Comes from Navajo Mountain."

April 3, 1882.
"Another Song Sung by Navajo Explorers." April 14, 1882.
"A Prospecting Party Goes to Monumental Valley." May 23, 1882.
"Too Fine to Save." December 23, 1892.
"Ledges of Mineral." December 30, 1892.
"One of the Hites." January 13, 1893.

Ross, William A. Deposition. August 3, 1882. Fort Defiance, Arizona Territory.

Rush, Jr., James M. "Interview." In *Great Sage Plain to Timberline: Our Pioneer History.* Volume IV. Cortez, Colorado: Montezuma County Historical Society, 2009.

Salt Lake Herald. "Way Down Upon the San Juan River." December 16, 1882.
"The Merrick Gold Mine." April 18, 1897.

Salt Lake Tribune. "Cass Hite on the San Juan." January 12, 1893.

Schurtz, George P. Letter to Charles Kelly. July 26, 1940. Charles Kelly Papers. Utah State Historical Society. Salt Lake City.

Shelton, W. T. Letter to John Wetherill. October 19, 1906. Otis R. "Dock" Marston Papers. Box 369, folder 19. The Huntington Library. San Marino, California.

Smith, Mrs. White Mountain. "Navajo Gold." *Desert Magazine.* November, 1938.

Spencer, Arthur H. "Lost Silver Mine of Monumental Valley." Unpublished manuscript. Otis R. "Dock" Marston Papers. Box 369, folder 19. The Huntington Library. San Marino, California.

Ssac (Cass Hite). "Peso-la-ki." *The Southwest* (Durango, Colorado). May 5, 1883. Alexander M. Stephen. Deposition. August 17, 1882. Keam's Canyon, Arizona Territory.

Sutherland, James R. Deposition. May 1, 1882. Fort Defiance, Arizona.

Terrell, John Upton. "Desert Folk Believe Ruess Killer Victim." *Salt Lake Tribune.* August 28, 1935.

The Southwest (Durango, Colorado). "From the Mancos." March 3, 1883.
No title. October 25, 1883.
"A Cave of Gold." December 1, 1883.

Times-Independent (Moab, Utah). "Interesting Career of Indian Scout, Pioneer Cattleman, Comes to a Close." May 31, 1934.

U. S. Bureau of the Census. "1880 Federal Census for the State of Colorado." Van Valkenburgh, Richard. "Monument Valley." *Arizona Highways.* April, 1940.

Warman, Cy. "The Peso-la-ki Mine." *Denver Republican.* July 18, 1897.
Frontier Stories. New York: Charles Scribner's Sons, 1898.

Watson, Edith L. "Golden Phantoms." *The Pueblo* (Colorado) *Indicator.* September 14, 1935.

Westcott, Winn. Personal interview with author. September 22, 2005. Monticello, Utah.

Wetherill, John. Testimony in River Bed Case, 1929-30. Utah State Historical Society. Salt Lake City.

Wetherill, Marion. Letter to Alice Brown. March 14, 1910. Copy in author's possession.

Williams, Jonathan P. Deposition. August 4, 1882. Territory of Arizona.

Williams, William F. "Statement of ...." May 22, 1929. Winslow, Arizona. Gladwell "Toney" Richardson Collection. Special

Collections, Cline Library. Northern Arizona University. Flagstaff.

Winslow, John R. "Gold Canyon." *True West*. July-August, 1966.

Yost, Billie Williams. *Bread Upon the Sands*. Caldwell, Idaho: The Caxton Publishers, Ltd., 1958.
Diamonds in the Desert. Flagstaff, Arizona: Silver Spruce Publishing, 1987.

Zoeller, Philip. Deposition. June 20, 1882. Fort Defiance, Arizona.